D1108414

GOLIATH

TOM GAULD

GOLIATH

DRAWN AND QUARTERLY BOOKS

MONTREAL

DRAWN & QUARTERLY
POST OFFICE BOX 48056
MONTREAL, QUEBEC
CANADA H2V 4S8
WWW.DRAWNANDQUARTERLY.COM

FIRST HARDCOVER EDITION: MARCH 2012
SECOND HARDCOVER PRINTING: MARCH 2012
PRINTED IN SINGAPORE
10 9 8 7 6 5 4 3 2

LIBRARY AND ARCHIVES CANADA
CATALOGUING IN PUBLICATION

GAULD, TOM
    GOLIATH / TOM GAULD

ISBN 978-1-77046-065-2

    I. GOLIATH (BIBLICAL GIANT)- COMIC BOOKS, STRIPS ETC.
I. TITLE

PN6737.G38G65 2011   741.5'9411   C2011-905293-8

DISTRIBUTED IN THE USA BY:
FARRAR, STRAUS AND GIROUX
18 WEST 18TH STREET
NEW YORK, NY 10011
ORDERS: 888.330.8477

DISTRIBUTED IN CANADA BY:
RAINCOAST BOOKS
2440 VIKING WAY
RICHMOND, BC V6V 1N2
ORDERS: 800.663.5714

DISTRIBUTED IN THE UK BY:
PUBLISHERS GROUP UK
8 THE ARENA, MOLLISON AVENUE
ENFIELD, EN3 7NL UNITED KINGDOM
ORDERS: 0208.804.0400

FOR JO

NOW THE PHILISTINES
GATHERED THEIR ARMIES
ON A MOUNTAIN AND
THE ARMIES OF ISRAEL
STOOD ON A MOUNTAIN
ON THE OTHER SIDE:
AND THERE WAS A
VALLEY BETWEEN THEM.

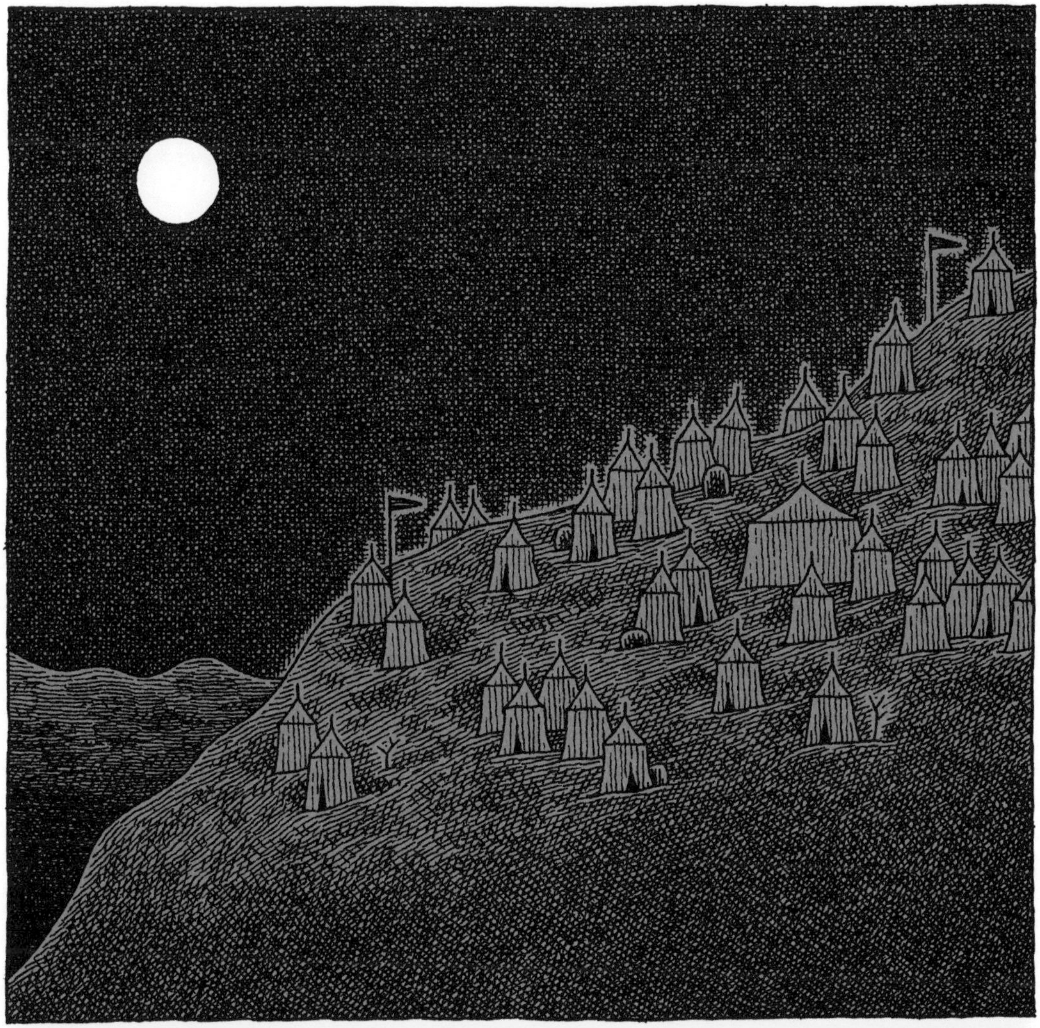

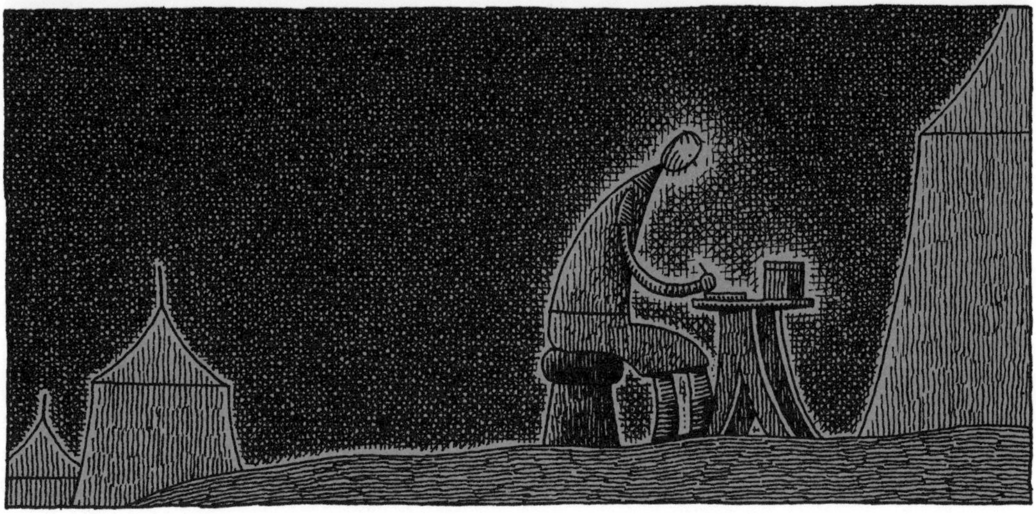

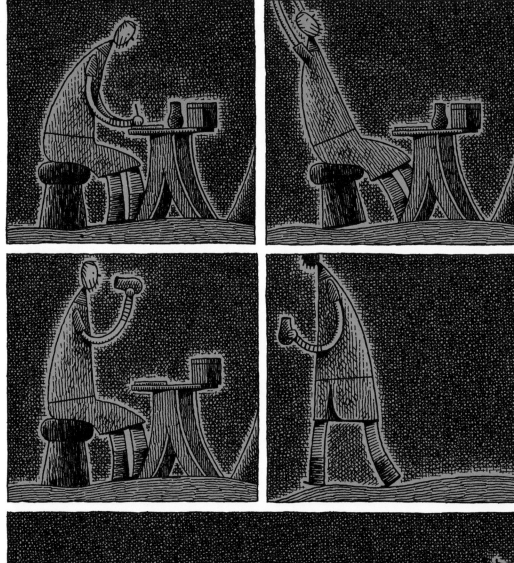

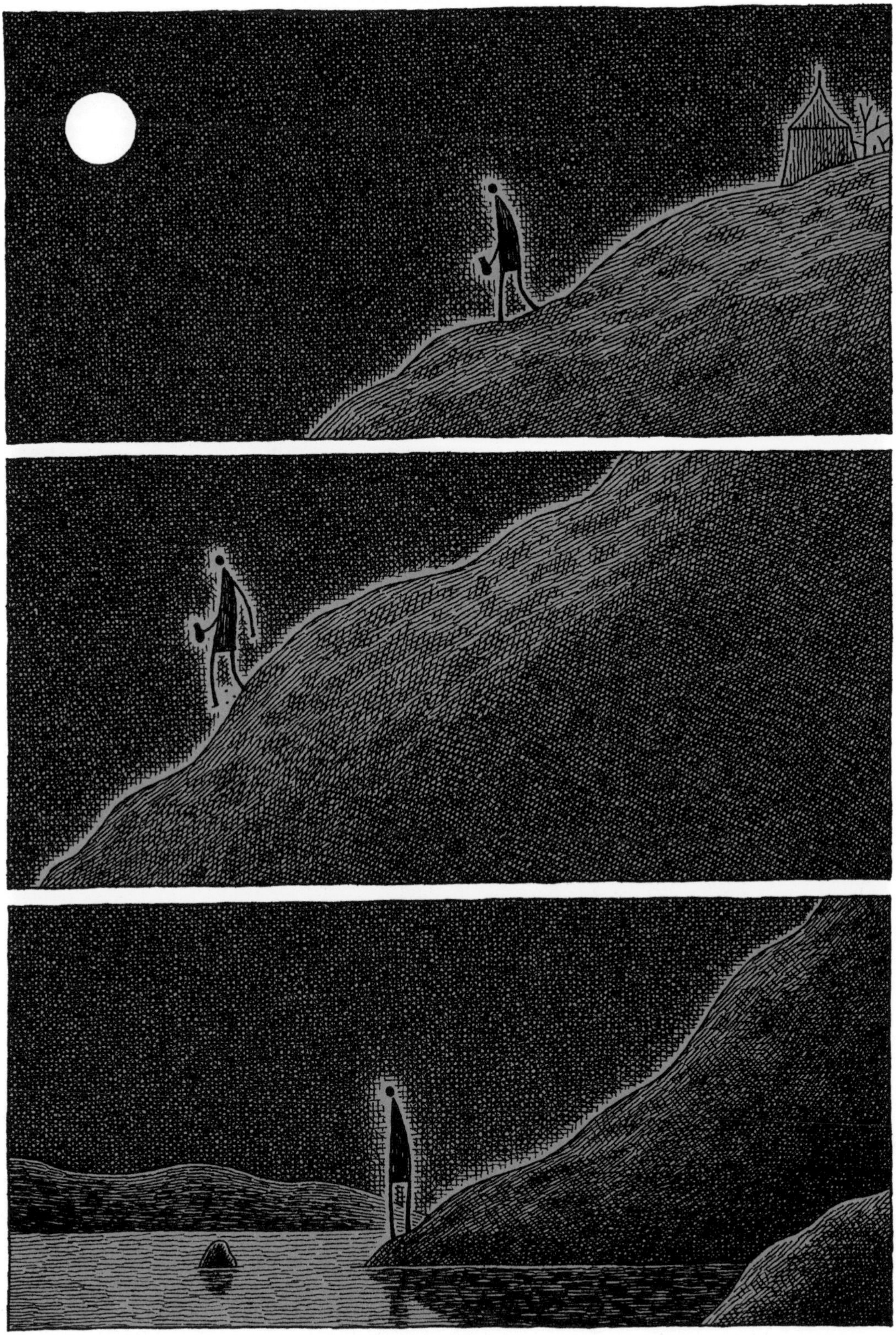

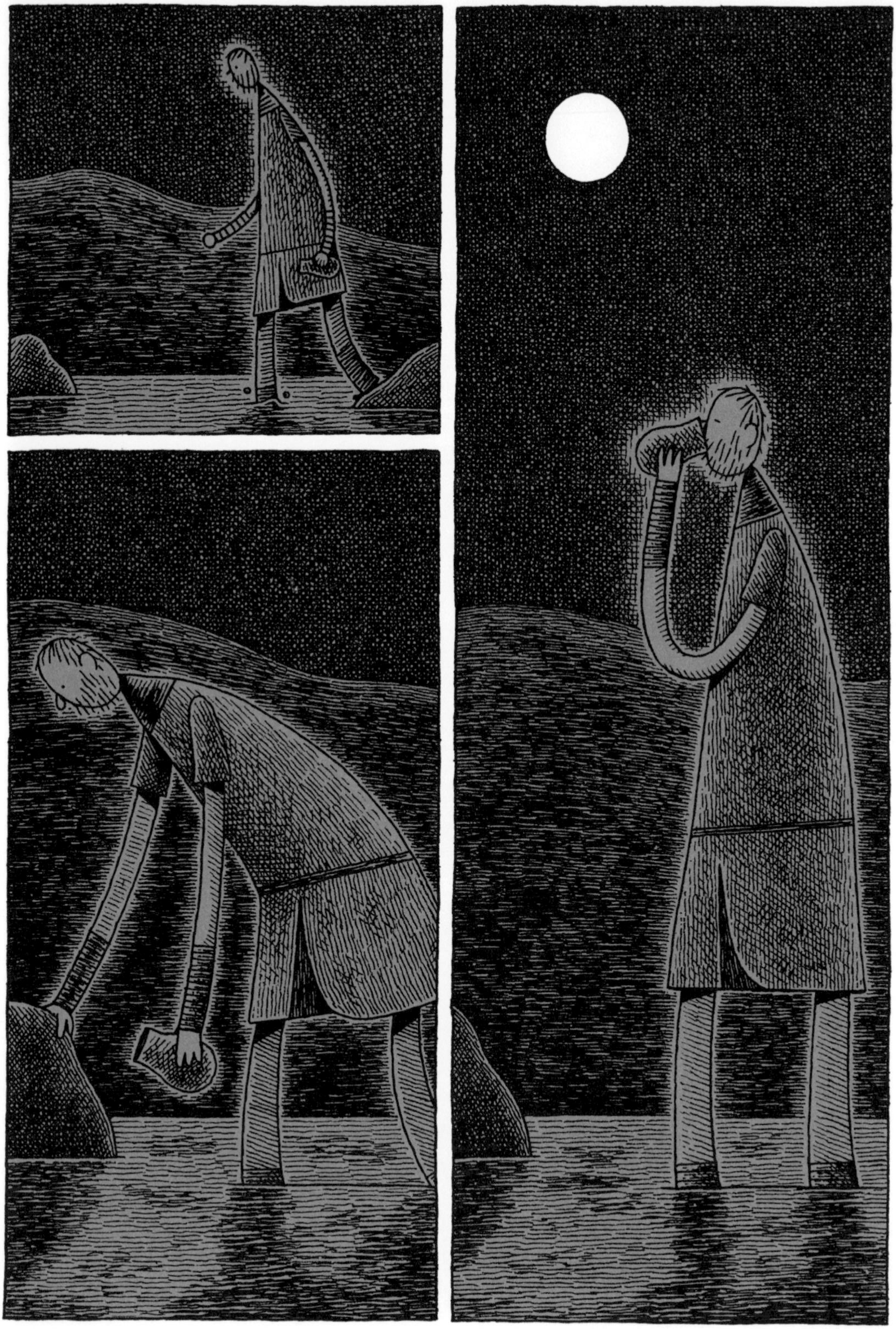

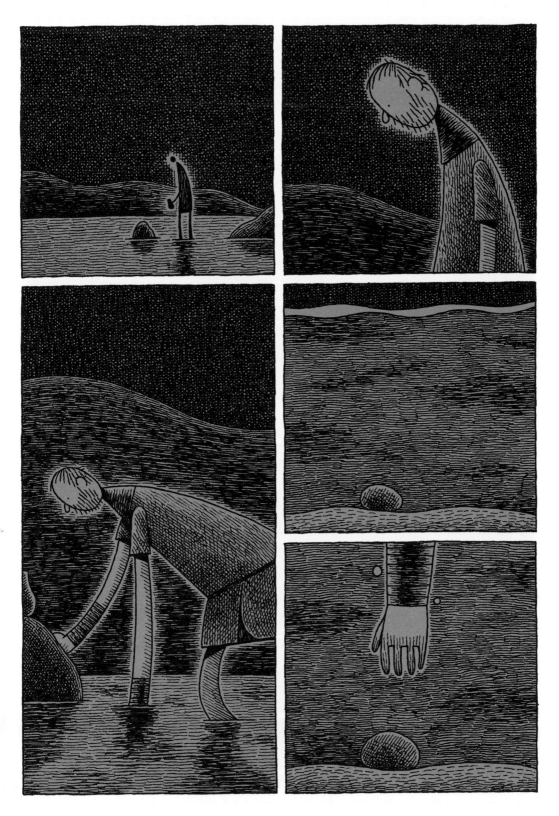

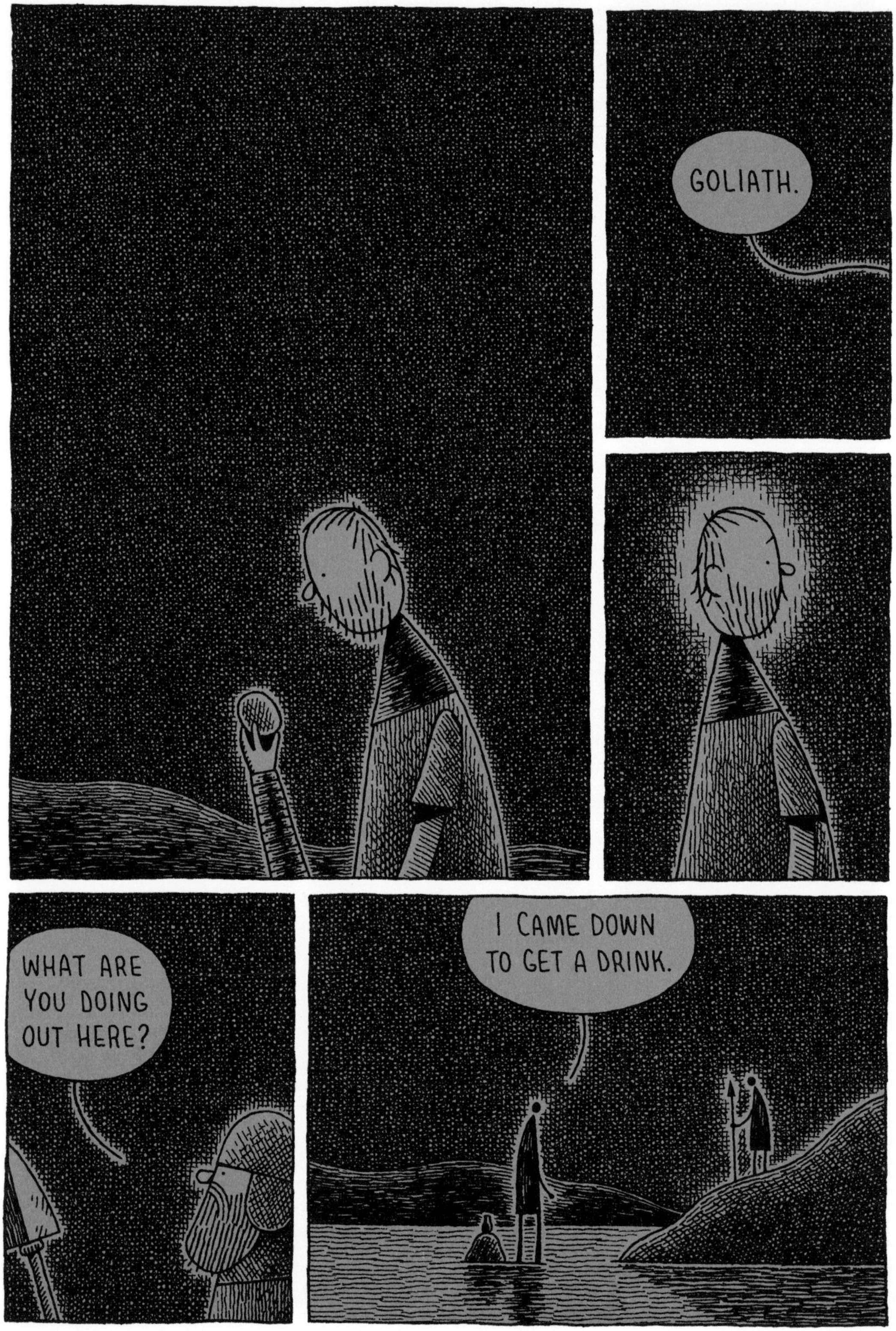
GOLIATH.
WHAT ARE YOU DOING OUT HERE?
I CAME DOWN TO GET A DRINK.

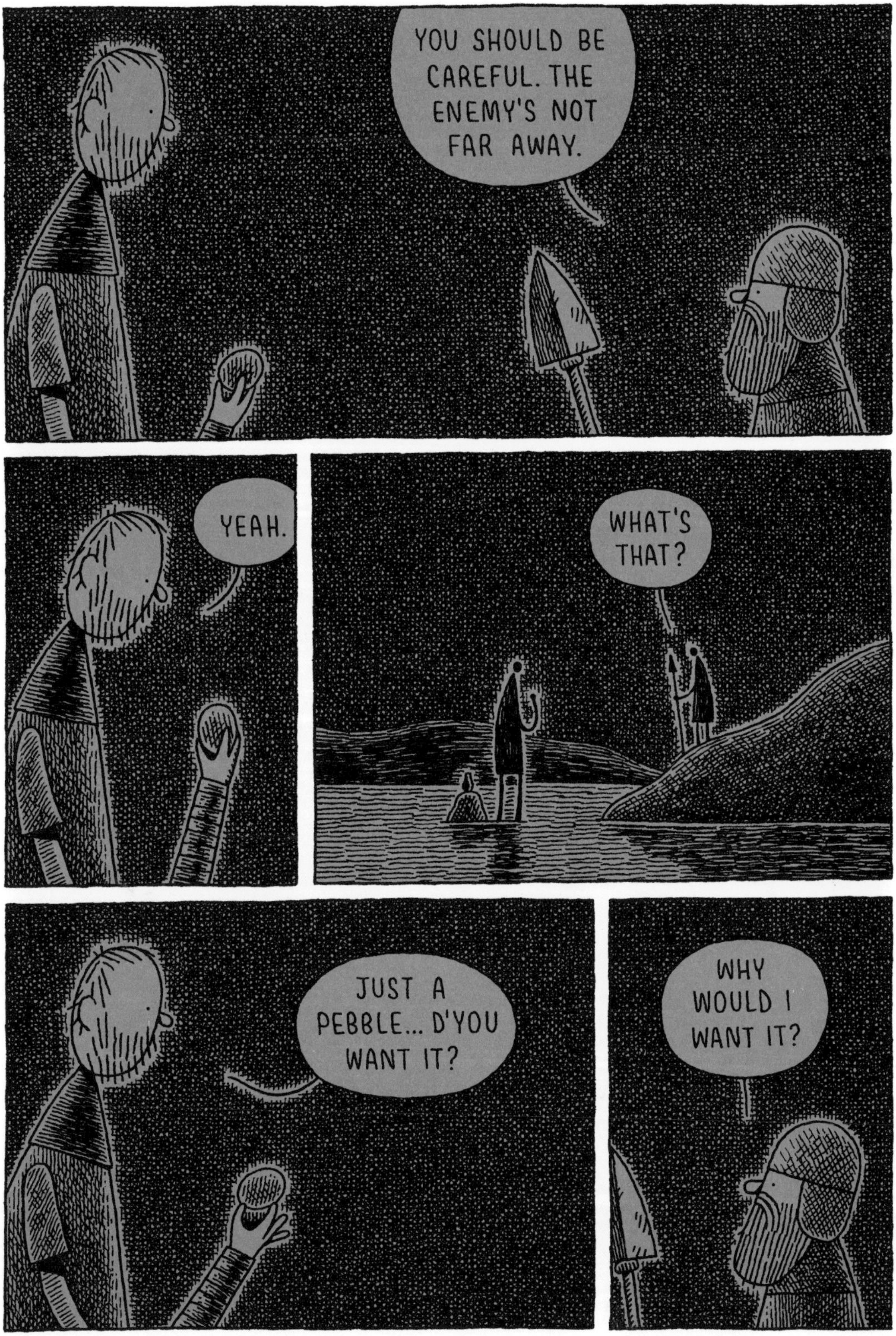
YOU SHOULD BE CAREFUL. THE ENEMY'S NOT FAR AWAY.
YEAH.
WHAT'S THAT?
JUST A PEBBLE... D'YOU WANT IT?
WHY WOULD I WANT IT?

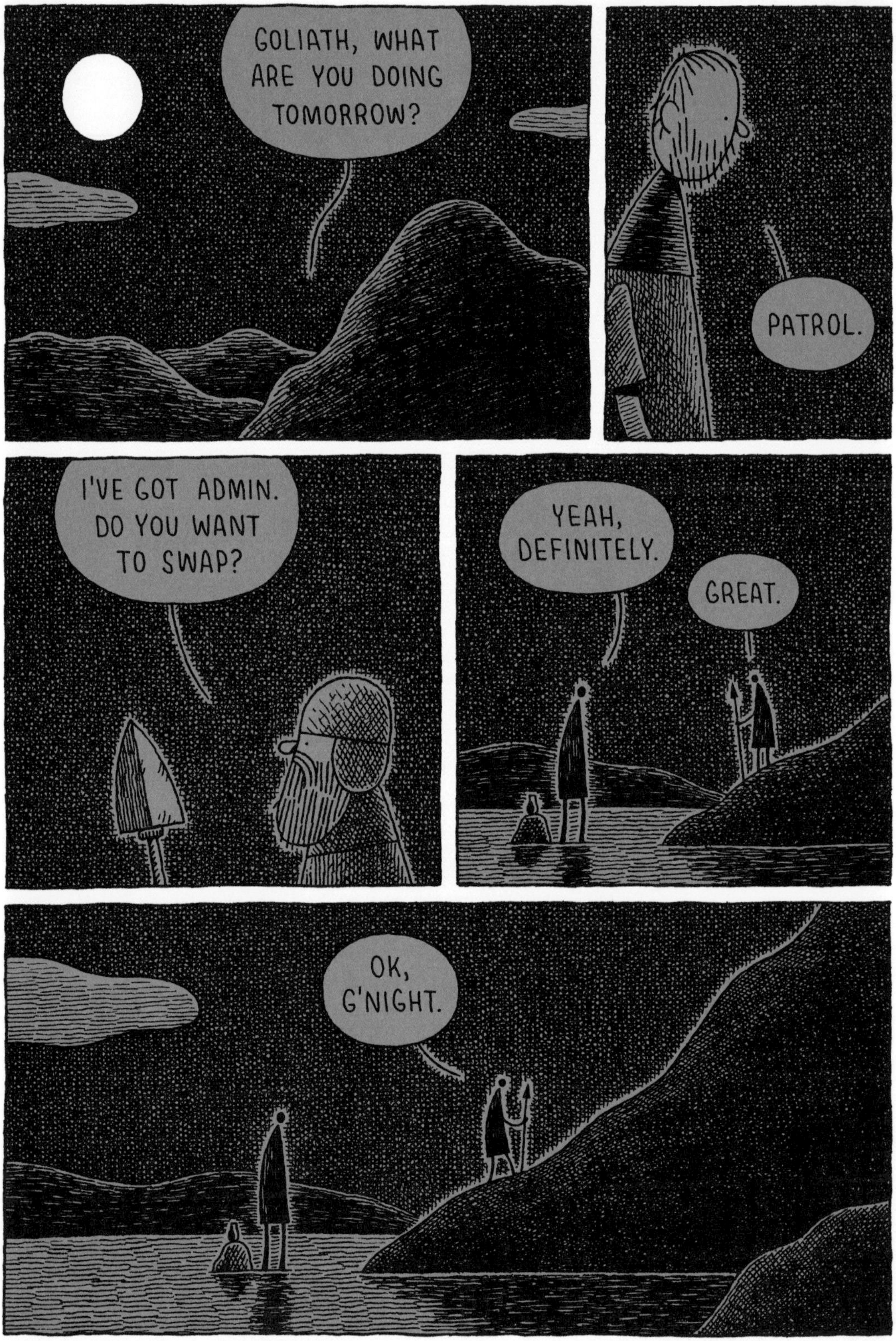
GOLIATH, WHAT ARE YOU DOING TOMORROW?
PATROL.
I'VE GOT ADMIN. DO YOU WANT TO SWAP?
YEAH, DEFINITELY.
GREAT.
OK, G'NIGHT.

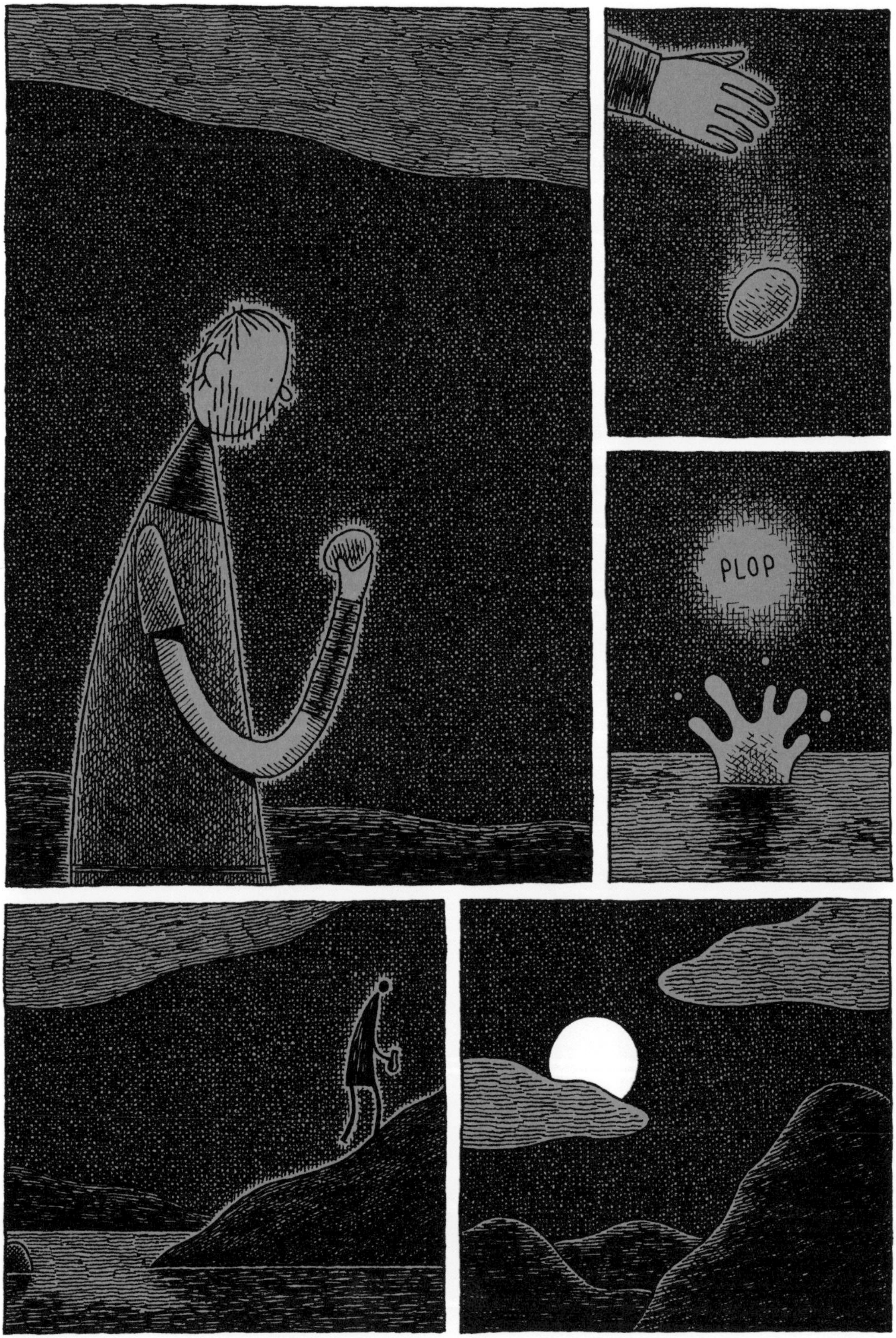
PLOP

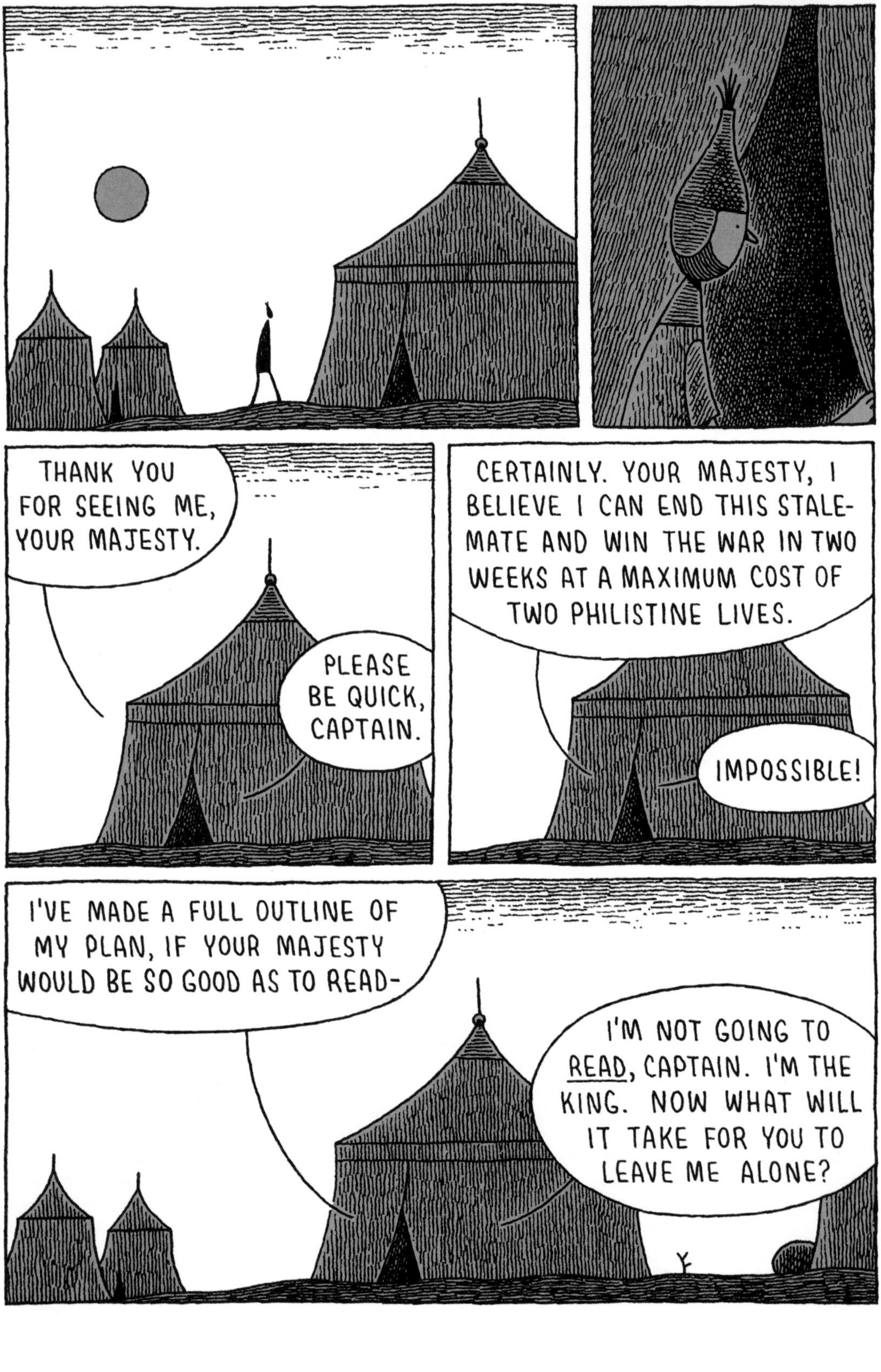
THANK YOU FOR SEEING ME, YOUR MAJESTY.
PLEASE BE QUICK, CAPTAIN.
CERTAINLY. YOUR MAJESTY, I BELIEVE I CAN END THIS STALE-MATE AND WIN THE WAR IN TWO WEEKS AT A MAXIMUM COST OF TWO PHILISTINE LIVES.
IMPOSSIBLE!
I'VE MADE A FULL OUTLINE OF MY PLAN, IF YOUR MAJESTY WOULD BE SO GOOD AS TO READ-
I'M NOT GOING TO READ, CAPTAIN. I'M THE KING. NOW WHAT WILL IT TAKE FOR YOU TO LEAVE ME ALONE?

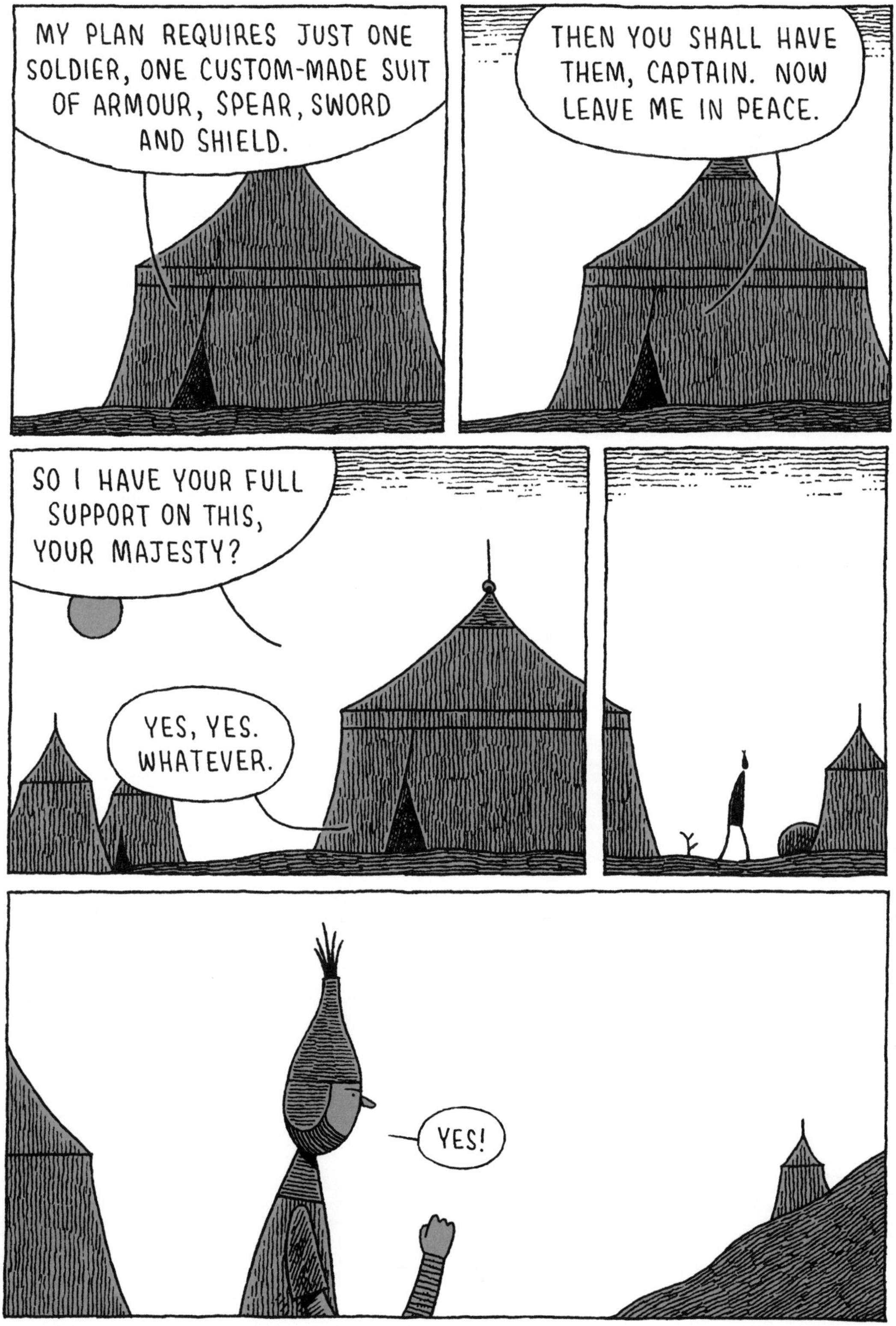
MY PLAN REQUIRES JUST ONE SOLDIER, ONE CUSTOM-MADE SUIT OF ARMOUR, SPEAR, SWORD AND SHIELD.
THEN YOU SHALL HAVE THEM, CAPTAIN. NOW LEAVE ME IN PEACE.
SO I HAVE YOUR FULL SUPPORT ON THIS, YOUR MAJESTY?
YES, YES. WHATEVER.
YES!

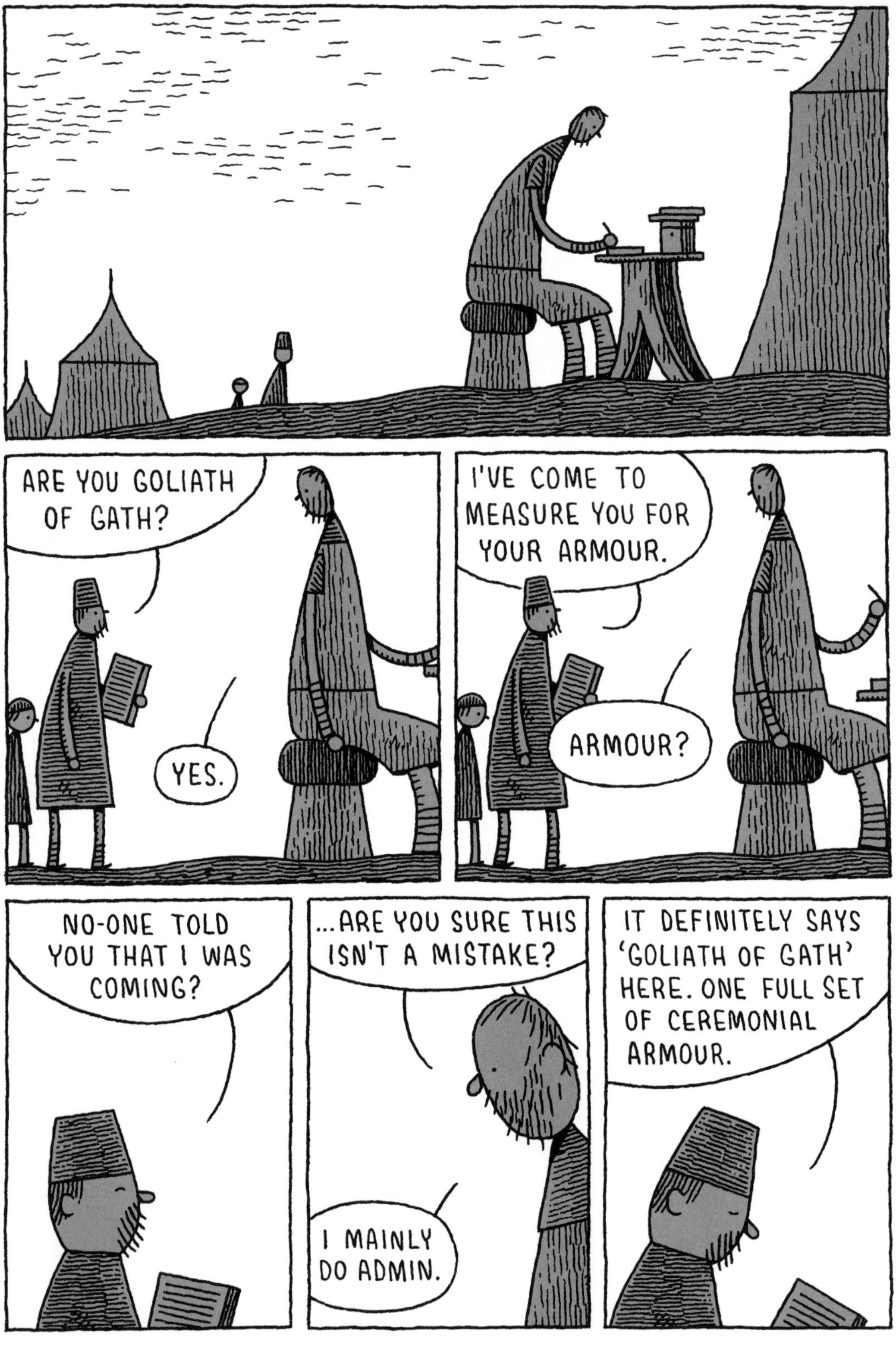
ARE YOU GOLIATH OF GATH?
YES.
I'VE COME TO MEASURE YOU FOR YOUR ARMOUR.
ARMOUR?
NO-ONE TOLD YOU THAT I WAS COMING?
...ARE YOU SURE THIS ISN'T A MISTAKE?
I MAINLY DO ADMIN.
IT DEFINITELY SAYS 'GOLIATH OF GATH' HERE. ONE FULL SET OF CEREMONIAL ARMOUR.

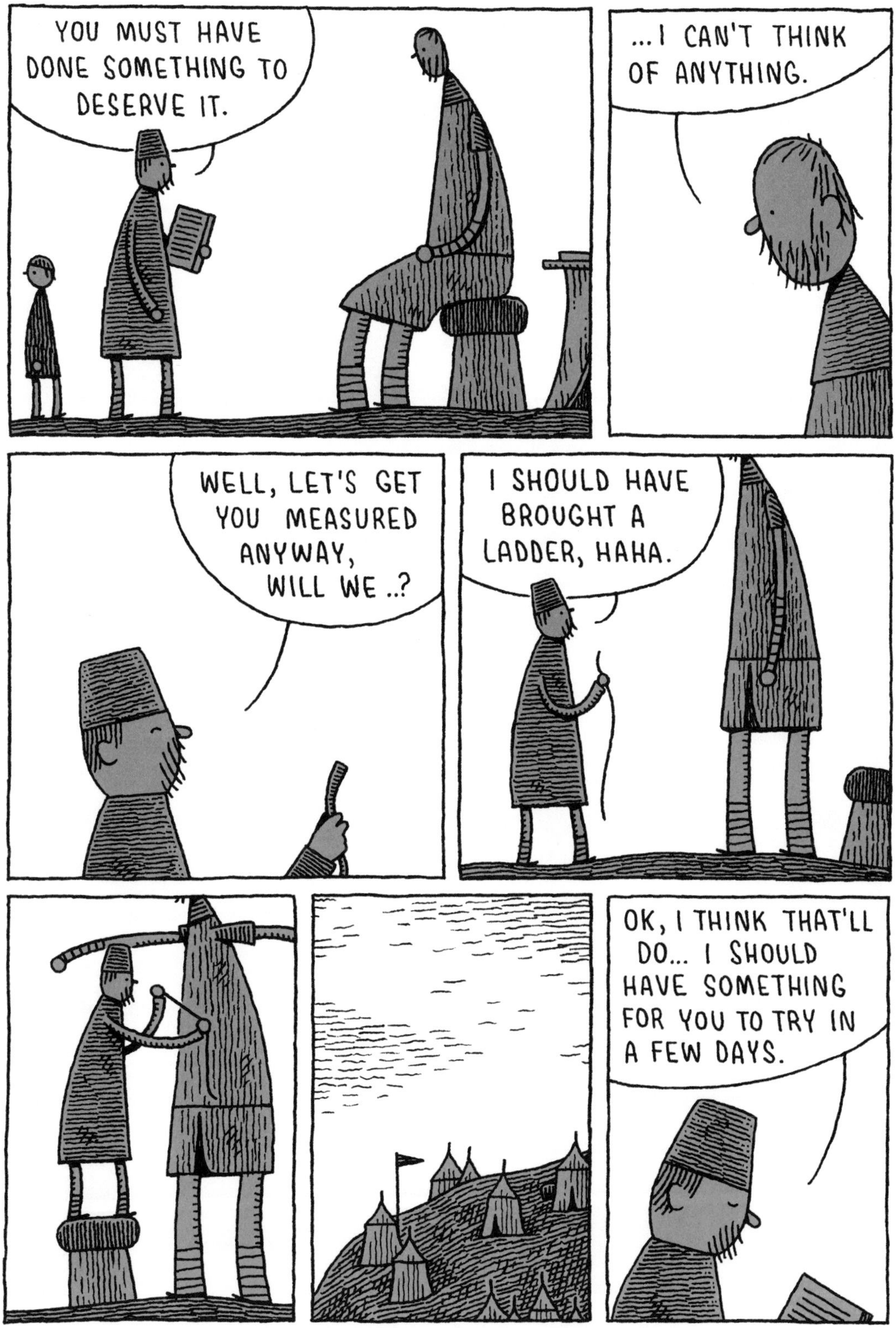
YOU MUST HAVE DONE SOMETHING TO DESERVE IT.
...I CAN'T THINK OF ANYTHING.
WELL, LET'S GET YOU MEASURED ANYWAY, WILL WE ..?
I SHOULD HAVE BROUGHT A LADDER, HAHA.
OK, I THINK THAT'LL DO... I SHOULD HAVE SOMETHING FOR YOU TO TRY IN A FEW DAYS.

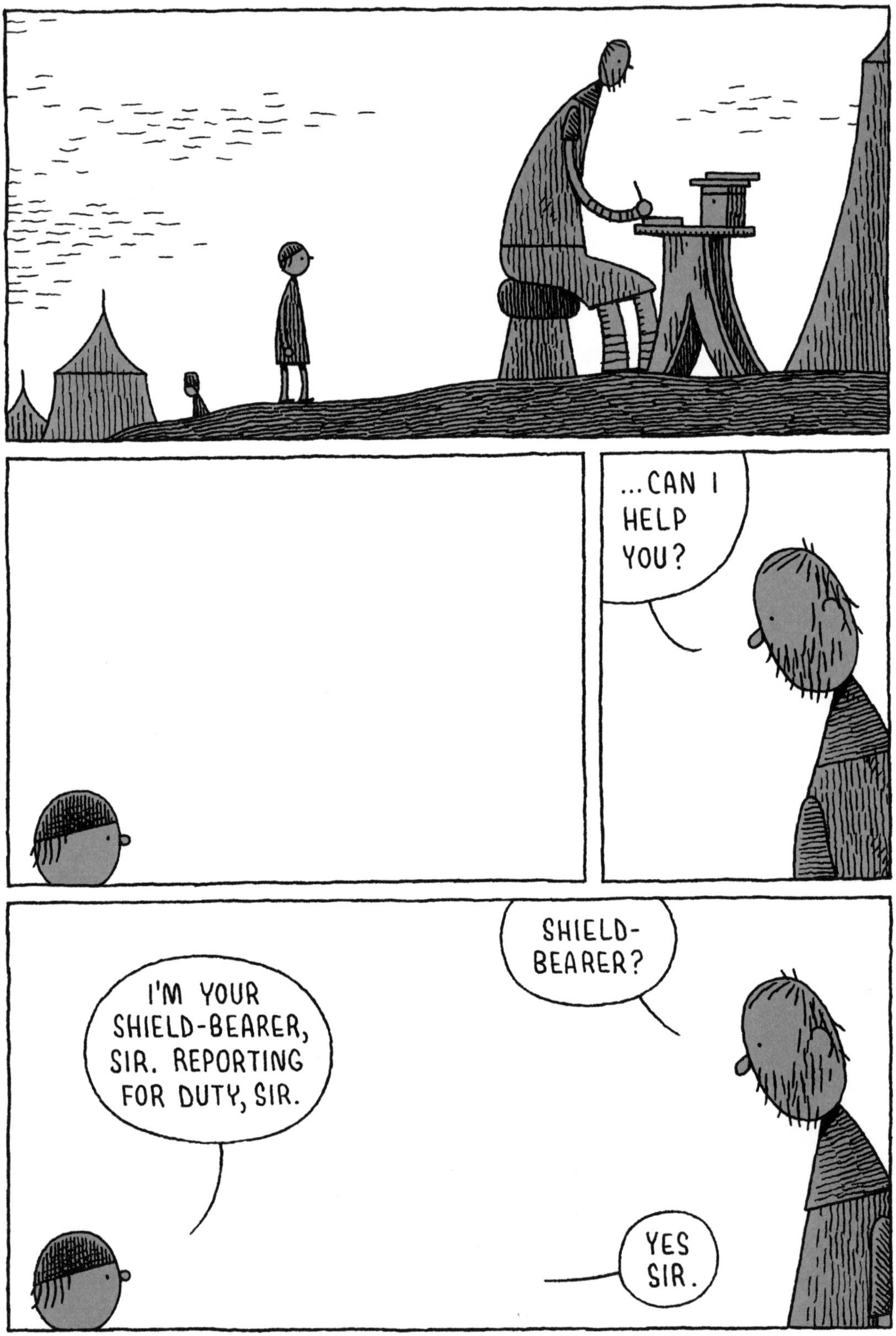
...CAN I HELP YOU?
I'M YOUR SHIELD-BEARER, SIR. REPORTING FOR DUTY, SIR.
SHIELD-BEARER?
YES SIR.

HOW OLD ARE YOU?
NINE, SIR.
SHOULDN'T YOU HAVE A SHIELD?
NOT YET, SIR. THEY'RE MAKING YOU A NEW ONE. AND A SWORD. AND A SPEAR.
I'M SUPPOSED TO TAKE YOU TO THE CAPTAIN.
OK, JUST LET ME PUT MY THINGS AWAY.

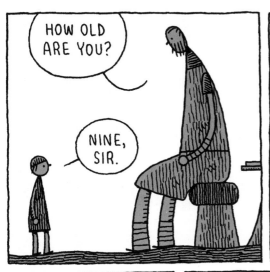

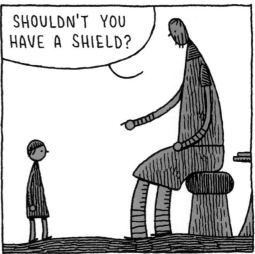

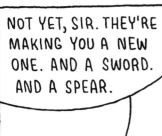

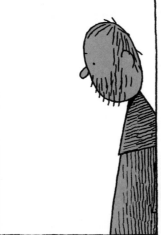

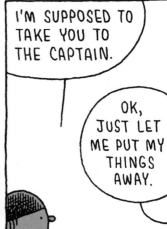

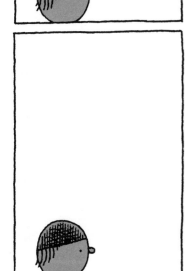

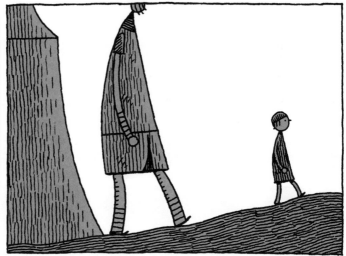

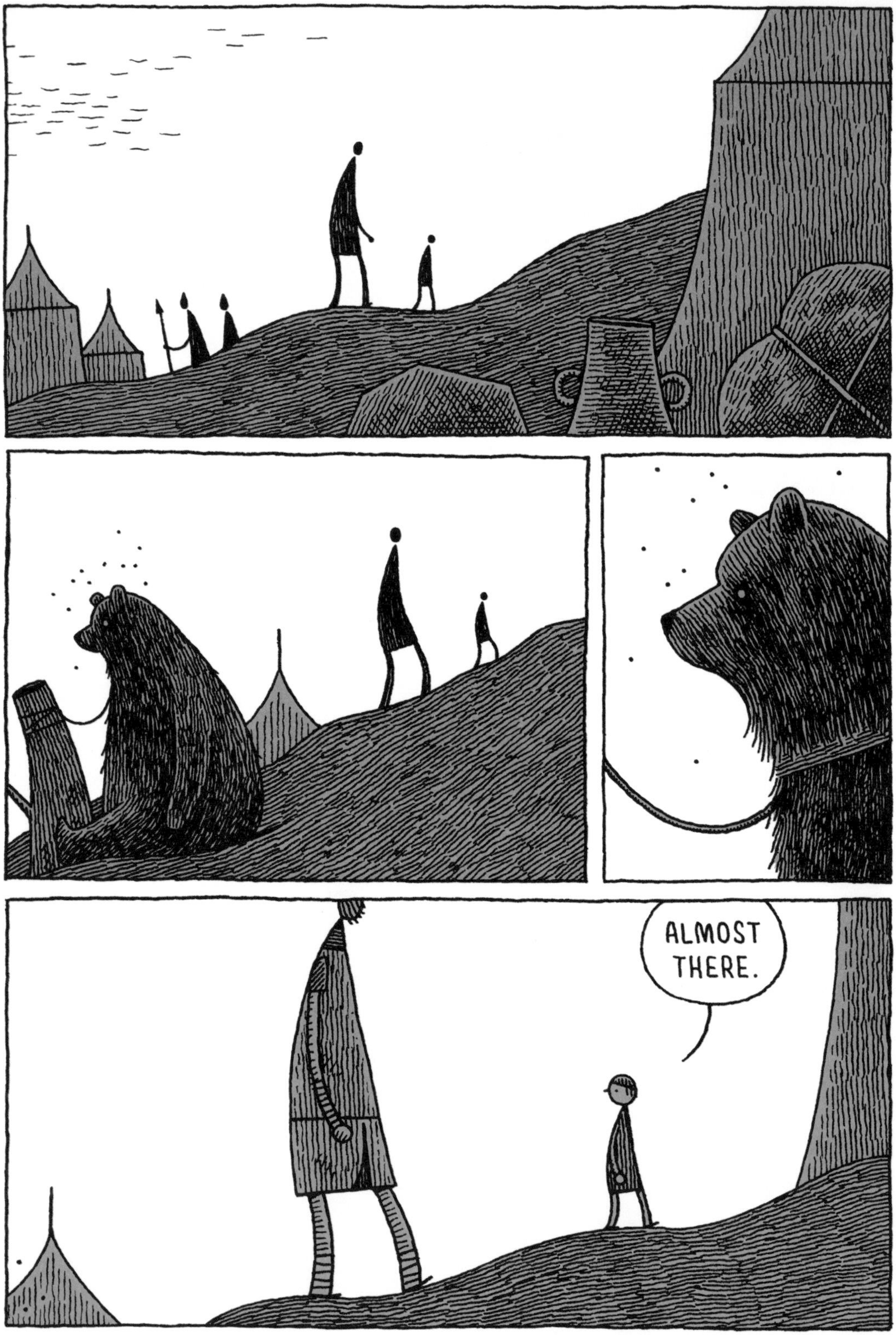
ALMOST THERE.

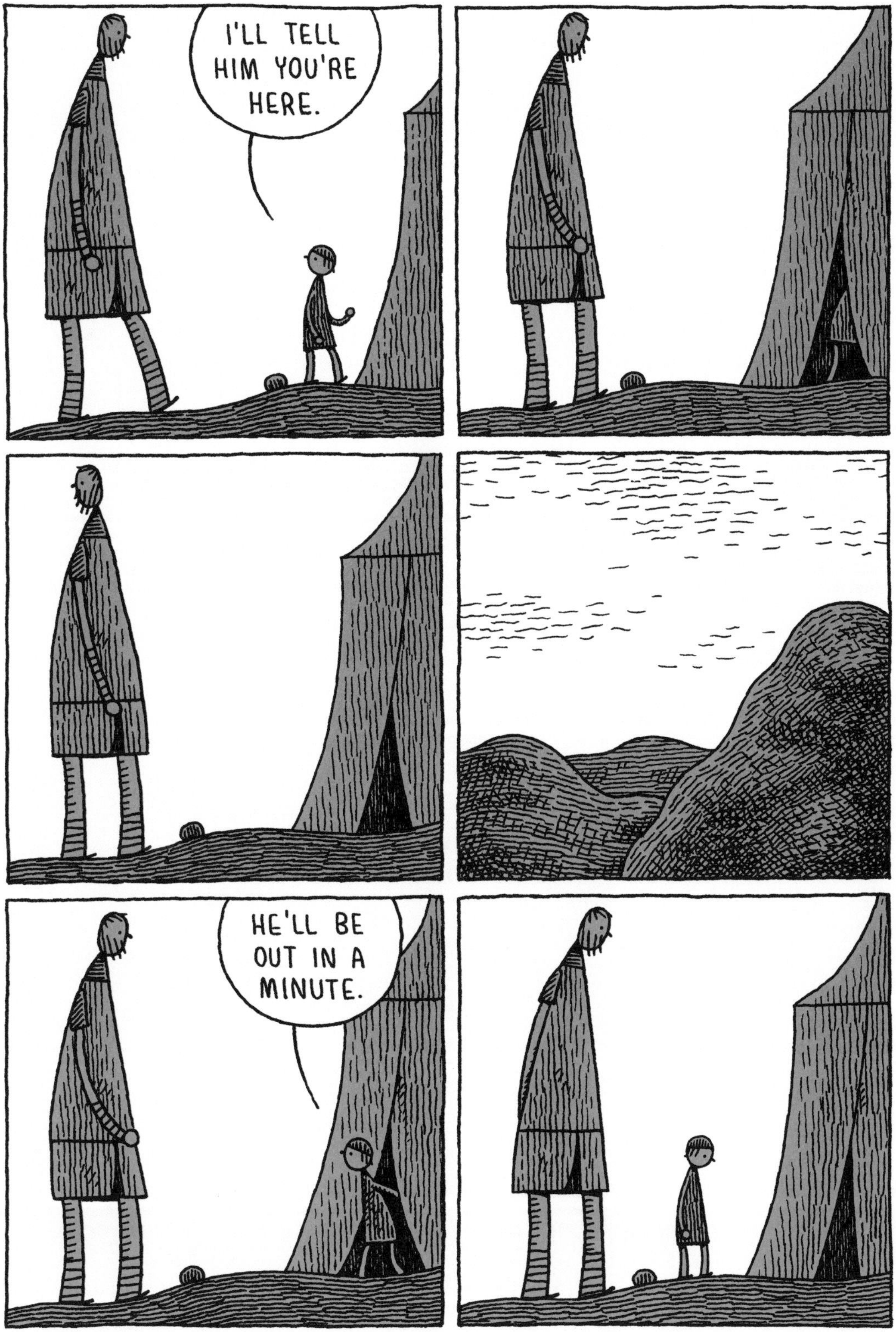
I'LL TELL HIM YOU'RE HERE.
HE'LL BE OUT IN A MINUTE.

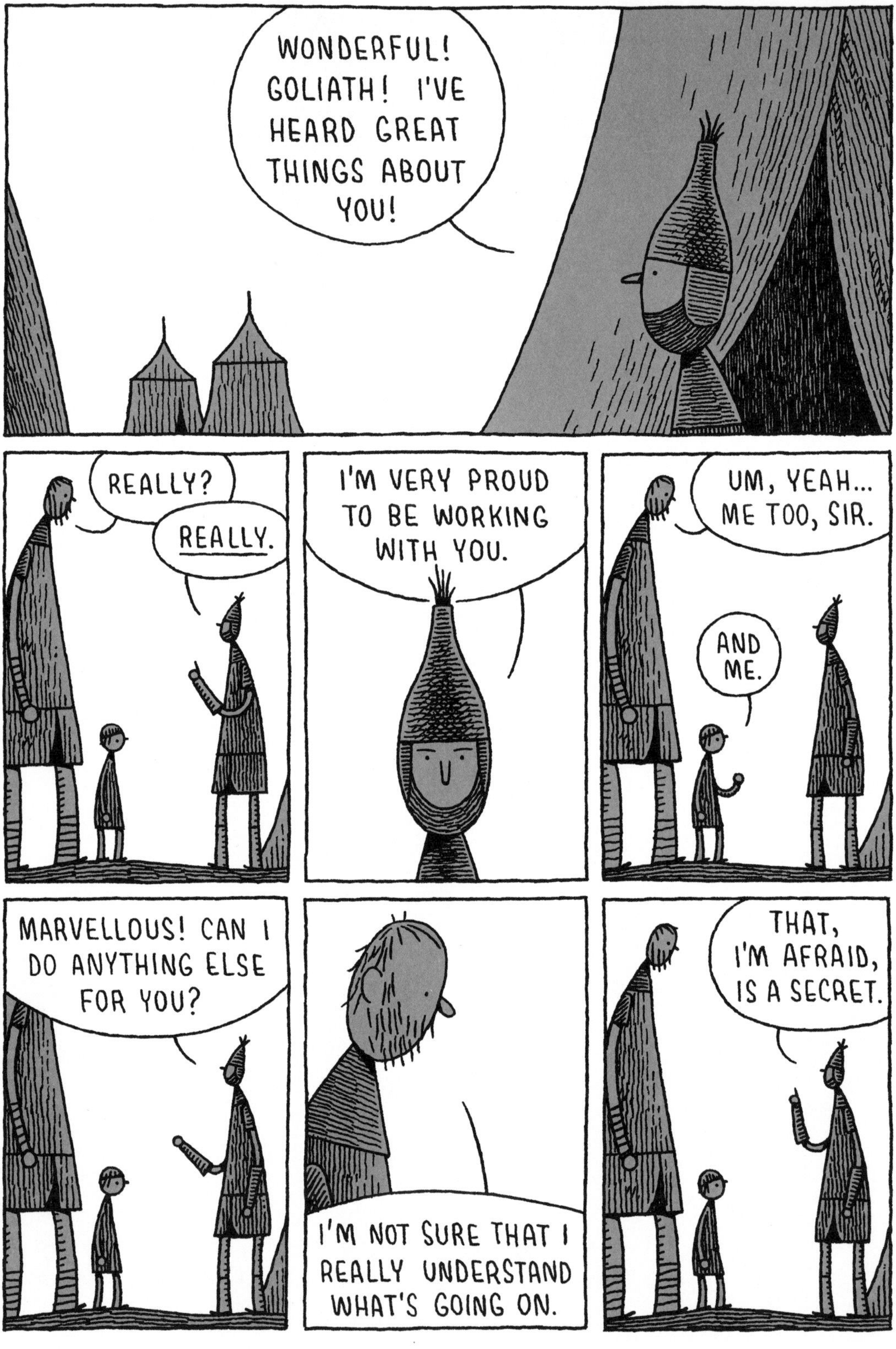
WONDERFUL! GOLIATH! I'VE HEARD GREAT THINGS ABOUT YOU!
REALLY?
REALLY.
I'M VERY PROUD TO BE WORKING WITH YOU.
UM, YEAH... ME TOO, SIR.
AND ME.
MARVELLOUS! CAN I DO ANYTHING ELSE FOR YOU?
I'M NOT SURE THAT I REALLY UNDERSTAND WHAT'S GOING ON.
THAT, I'M AFRAID, IS A SECRET.

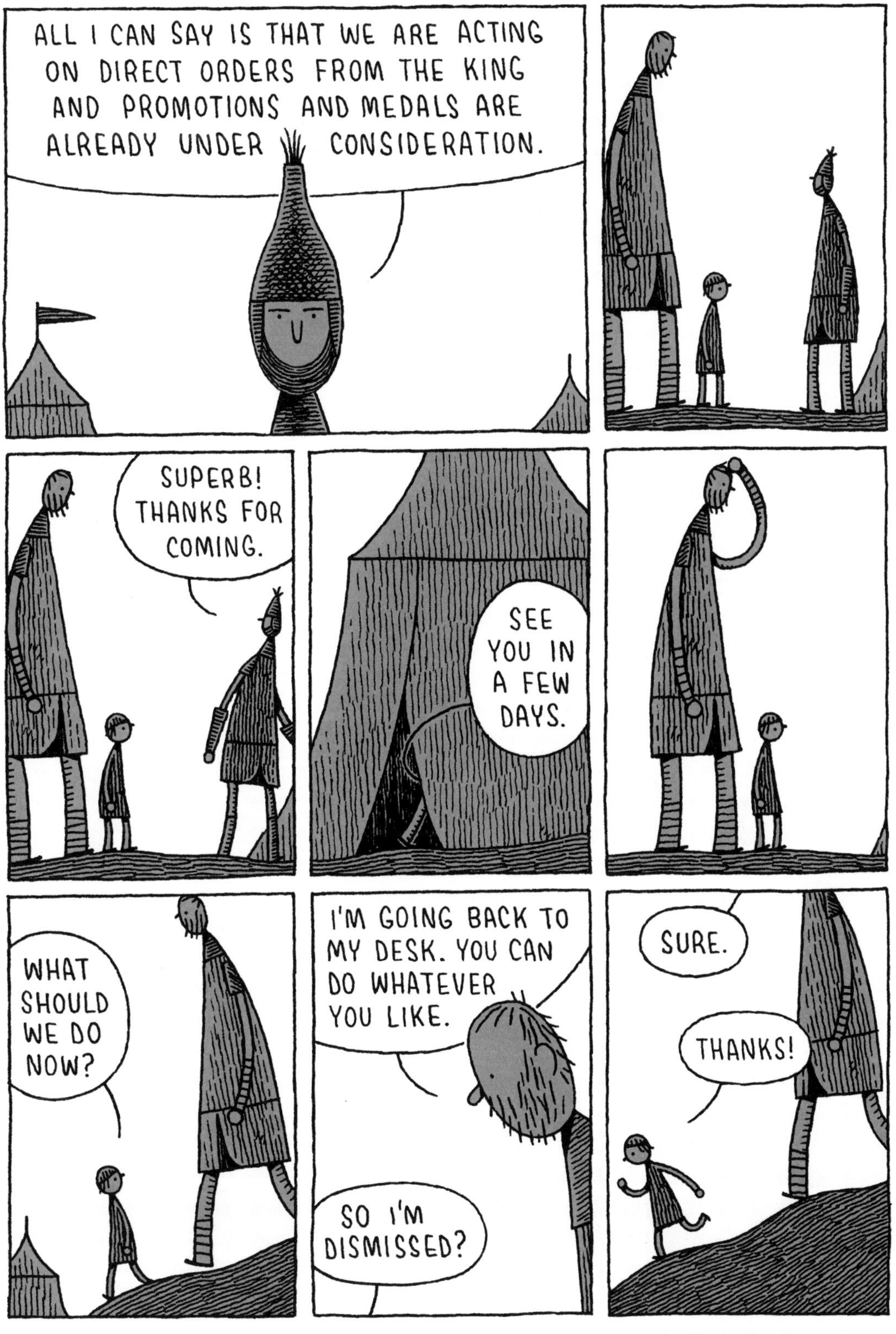
ALL I CAN SAY IS THAT WE ARE ACTING ON DIRECT ORDERS FROM THE KING AND PROMOTIONS AND MEDALS ARE ALREADY UNDER CONSIDERATION.
SUPERB! THANKS FOR COMING.
SEE YOU IN A FEW DAYS.
WHAT SHOULD WE DO NOW?
I'M GOING BACK TO MY DESK. YOU CAN DO WHATEVER YOU LIKE.
SO I'M DISMISSED?
SURE.
THANKS!

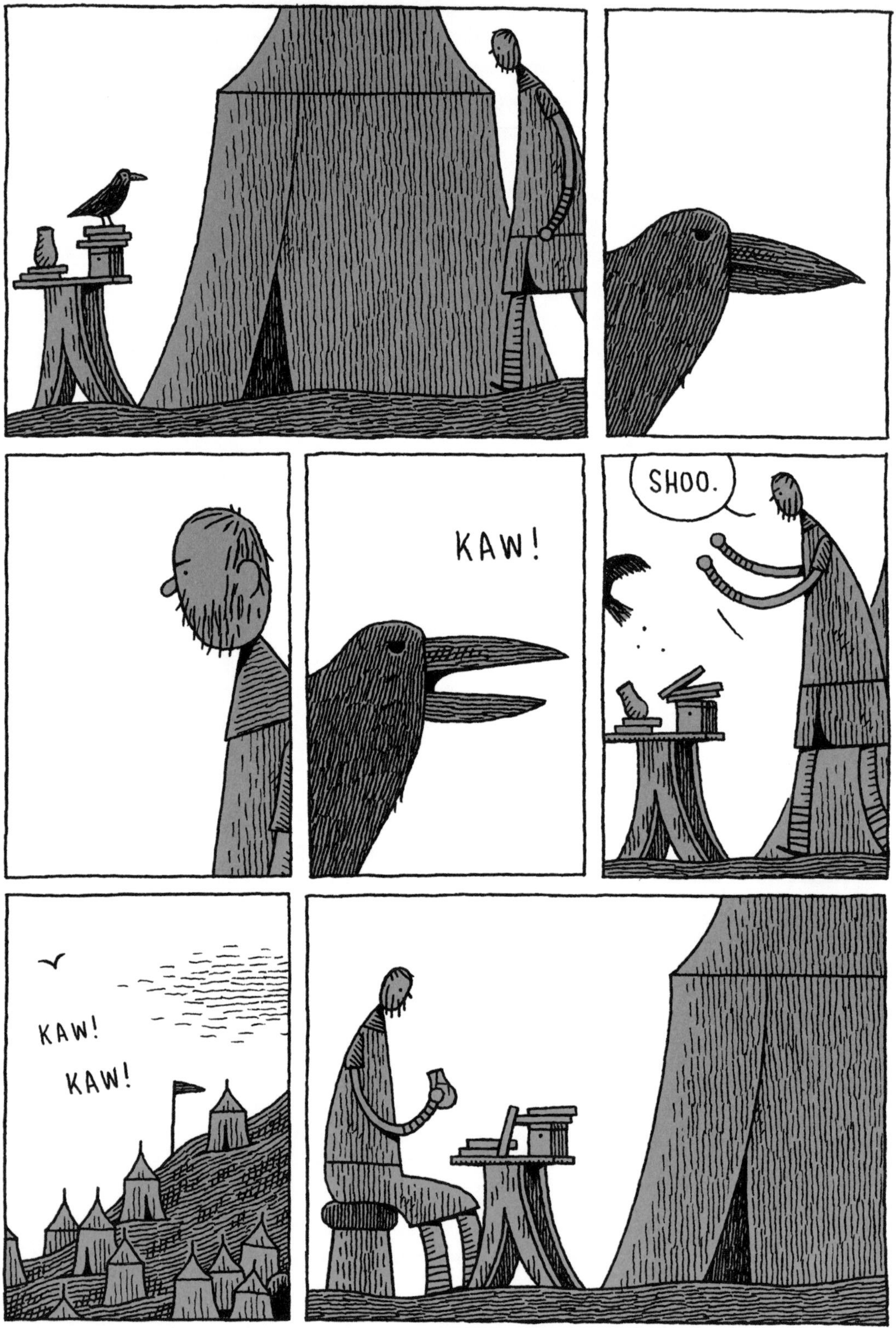
KAW!
SHOO.
KAW!
KAW!

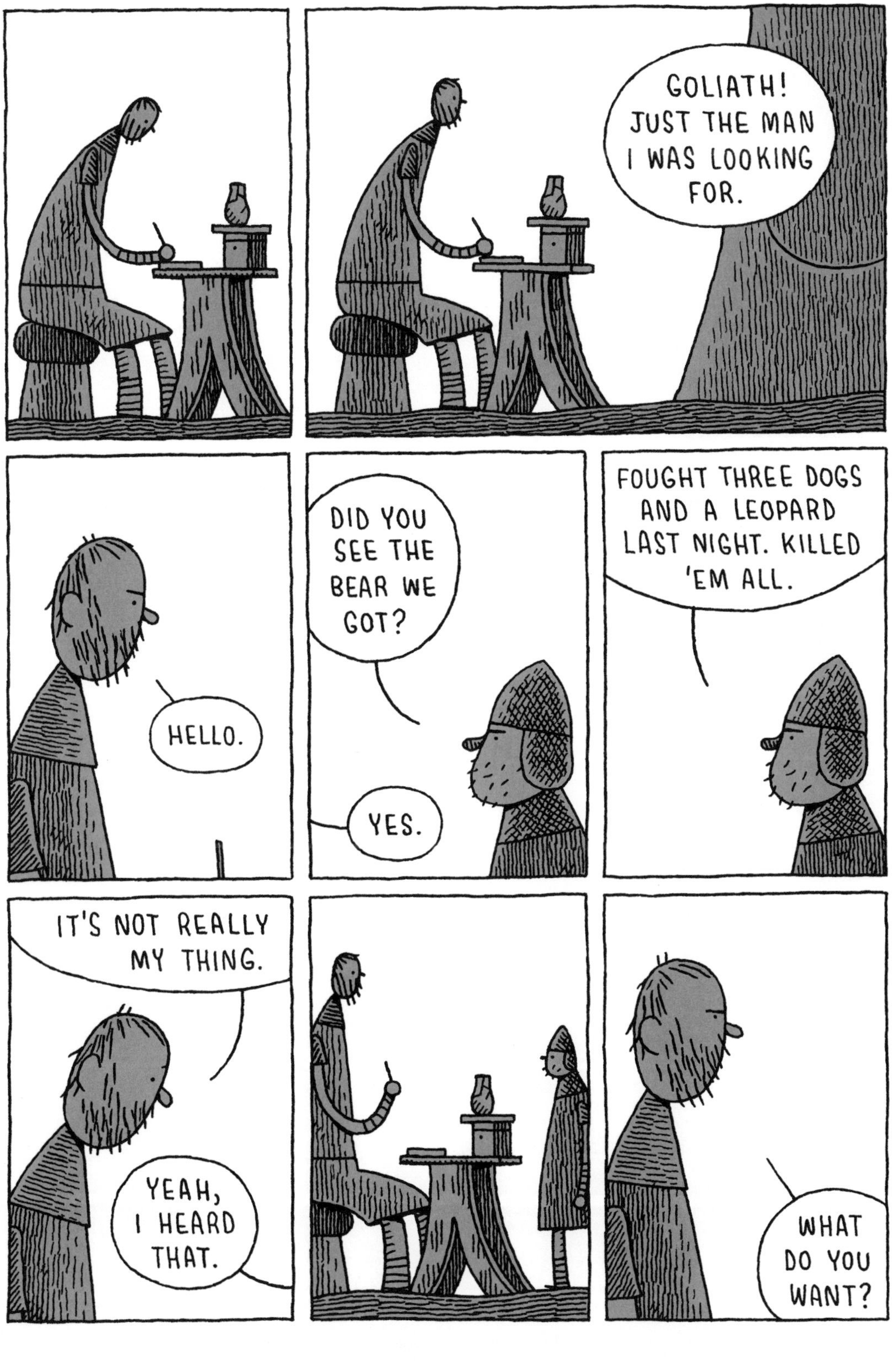
GOLIATH! JUST THE MAN I WAS LOOKING FOR.
HELLO.
DID YOU SEE THE BEAR WE GOT?
YES.
FOUGHT THREE DOGS AND A LEOPARD LAST NIGHT. KILLED 'EM ALL.
IT'S NOT REALLY MY THING.
YEAH, I HEARD THAT.
WHAT DO YOU WANT?

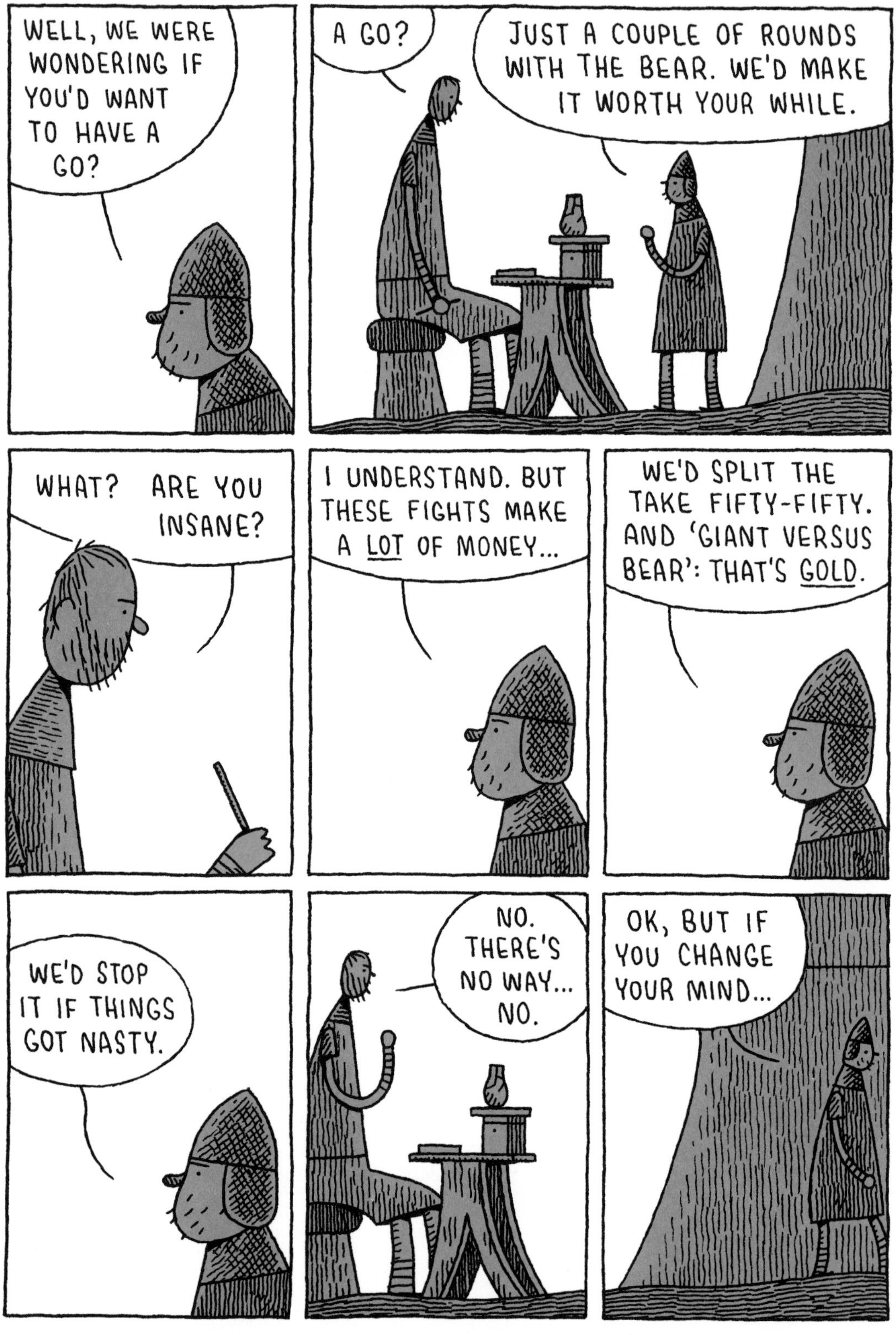
WELL, WE WERE WONDERING IF YOU'D WANT TO HAVE A GO?
A GO?
JUST A COUPLE OF ROUNDS WITH THE BEAR. WE'D MAKE IT WORTH YOUR WHILE.
WHAT? ARE YOU INSANE?
I UNDERSTAND. BUT THESE FIGHTS MAKE A LOT OF MONEY...
WE'D SPLIT THE TAKE FIFTY-FIFTY. AND 'GIANT VERSUS BEAR': THAT'S GOLD.
WE'D STOP IT IF THINGS GOT NASTY.
NO. THERE'S NO WAY... NO.
OK, BUT IF YOU CHANGE YOUR MIND...

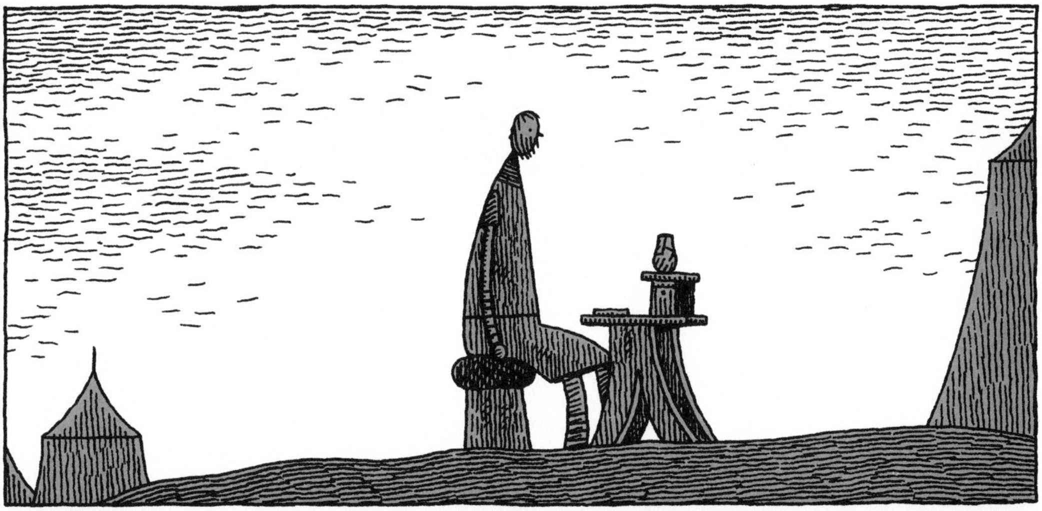
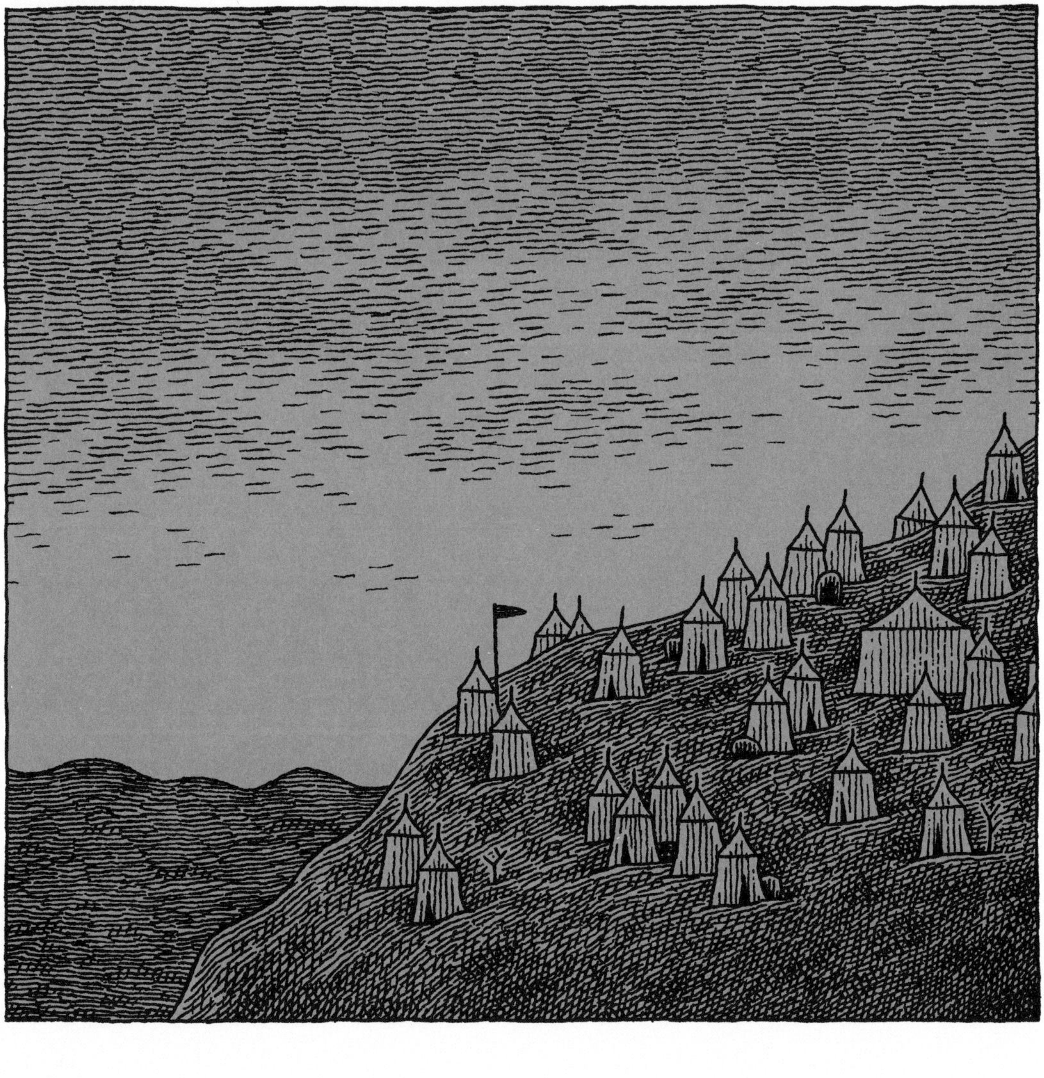

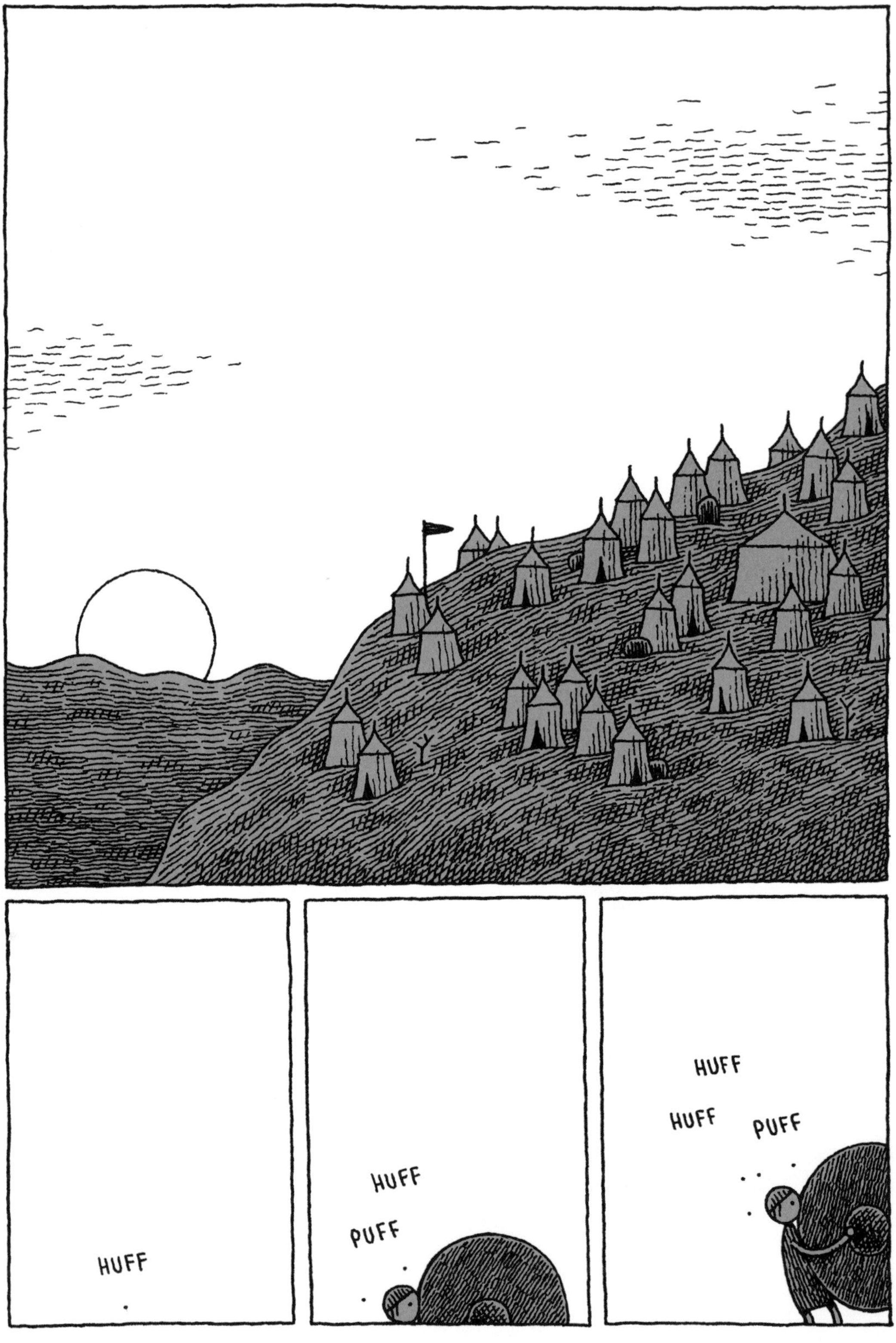
HUFF
HUFF
PUFF
HUFF
HUFF
PUFF

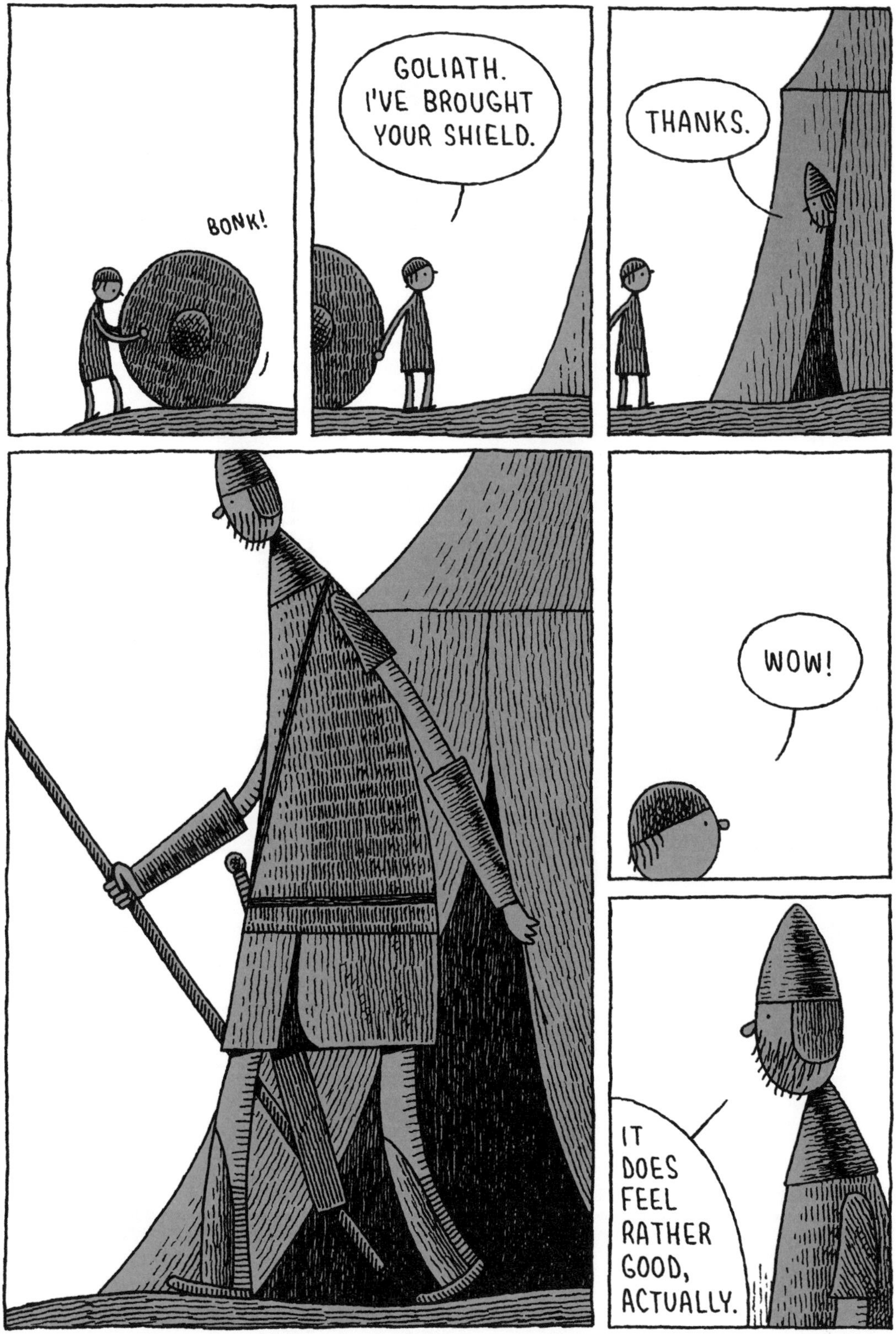
BONK!
GOLIATH. I'VE BROUGHT YOUR SHIELD.
THANKS.
WOW!
IT DOES FEEL RATHER GOOD, ACTUALLY.

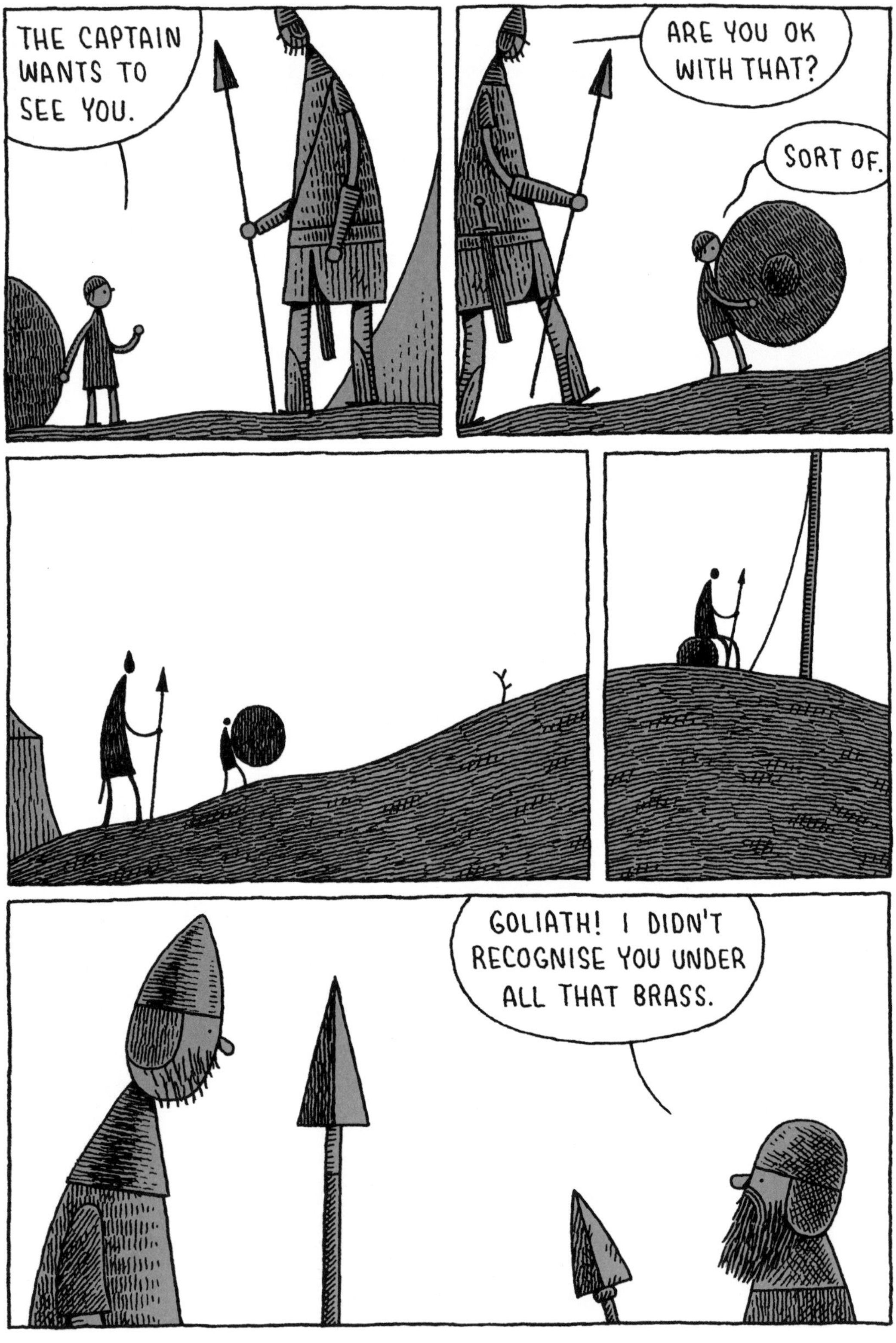
THE CAPTAIN WANTS TO SEE YOU.
ARE YOU OK WITH THAT?
SORT OF.
GOLIATH! I DIDN'T RECOGNISE YOU UNDER ALL THAT BRASS.

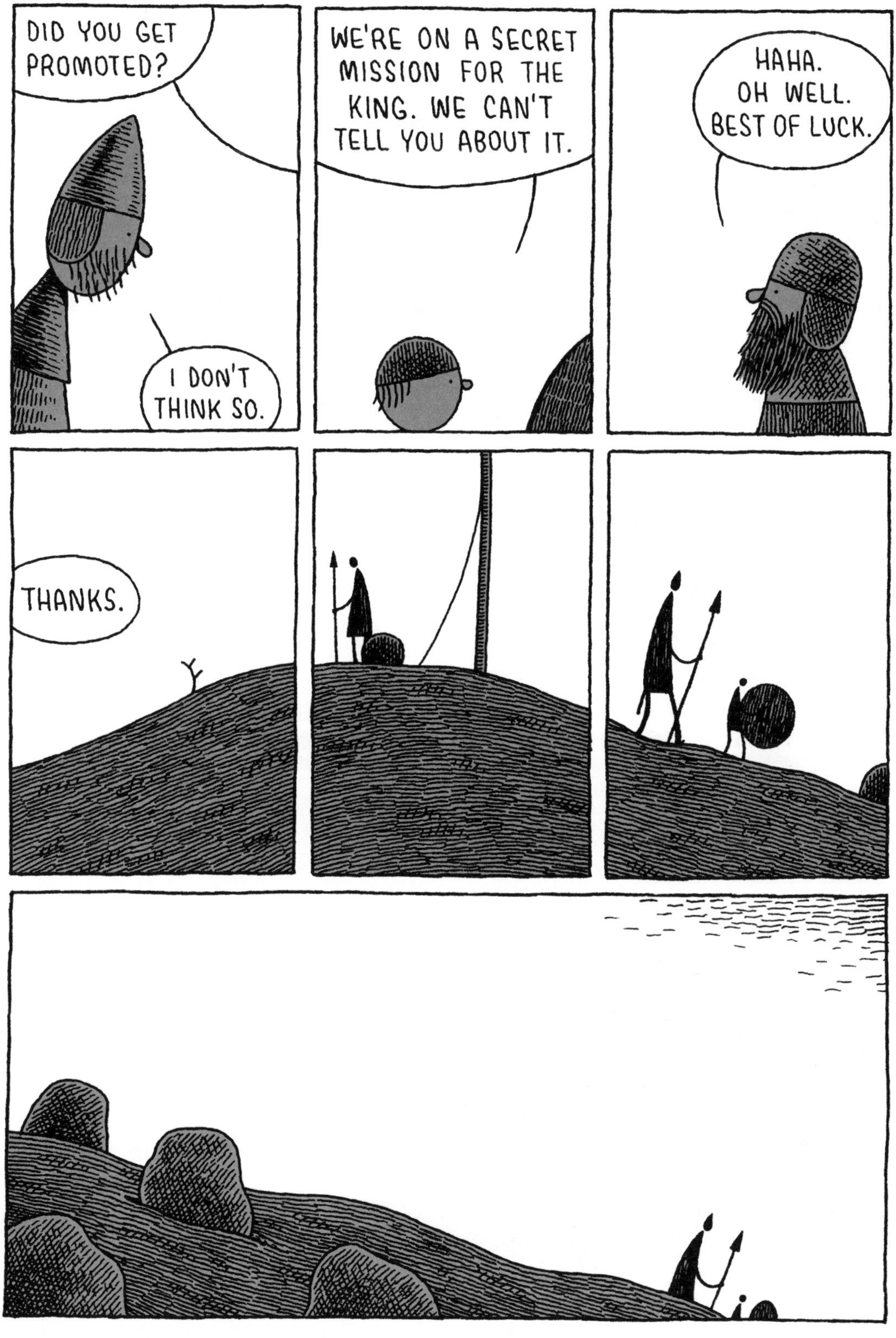
DID YOU GET PROMOTED?
I DON'T THINK SO.
WE'RE ON A SECRET MISSION FOR THE KING. WE CAN'T TELL YOU ABOUT IT.
HAHA. OH WELL. BEST OF LUCK.
THANKS.

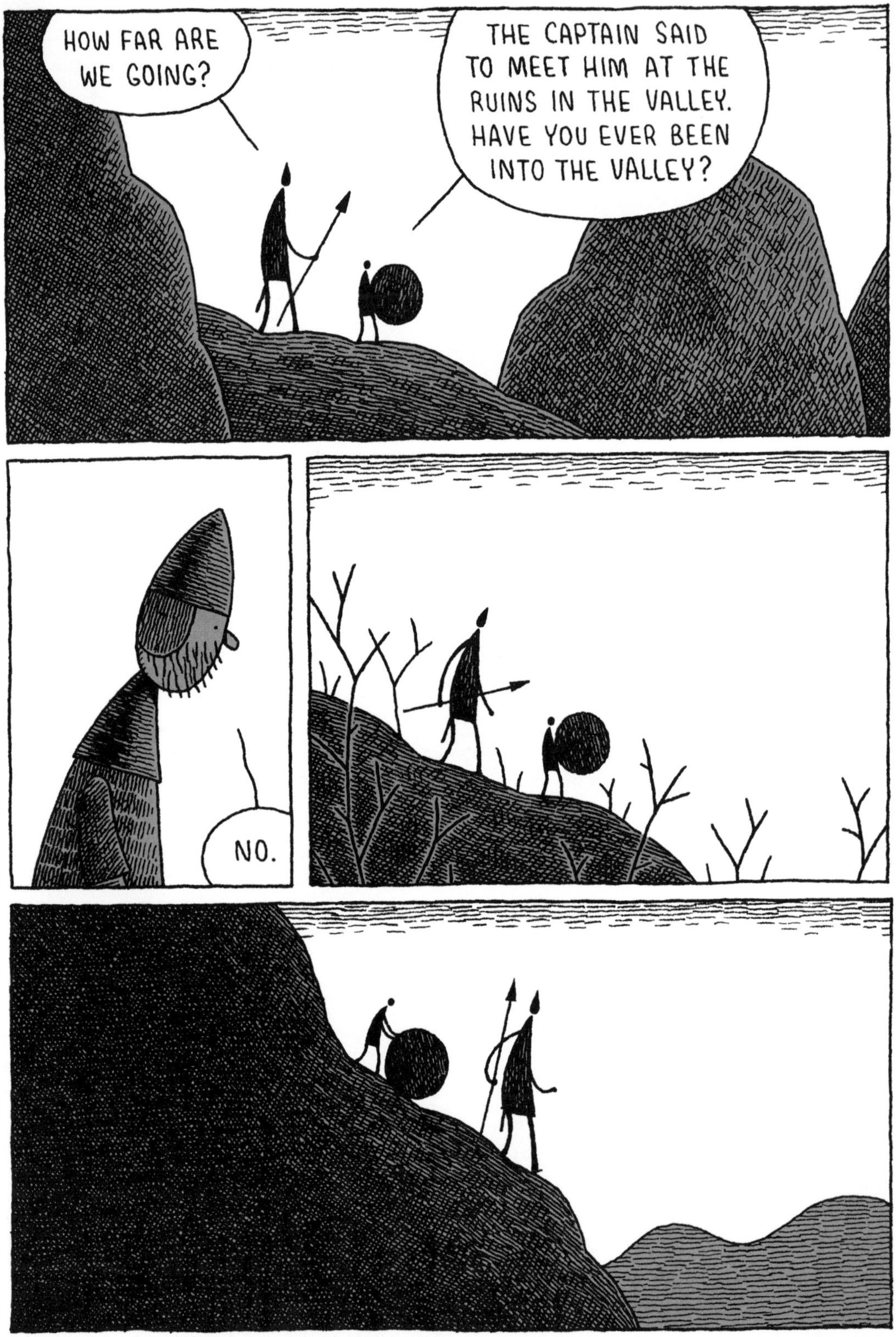
HOW FAR ARE WE GOING?
THE CAPTAIN SAID TO MEET HIM AT THE RUINS IN THE VALLEY. HAVE YOU EVER BEEN INTO THE VALLEY?
NO.

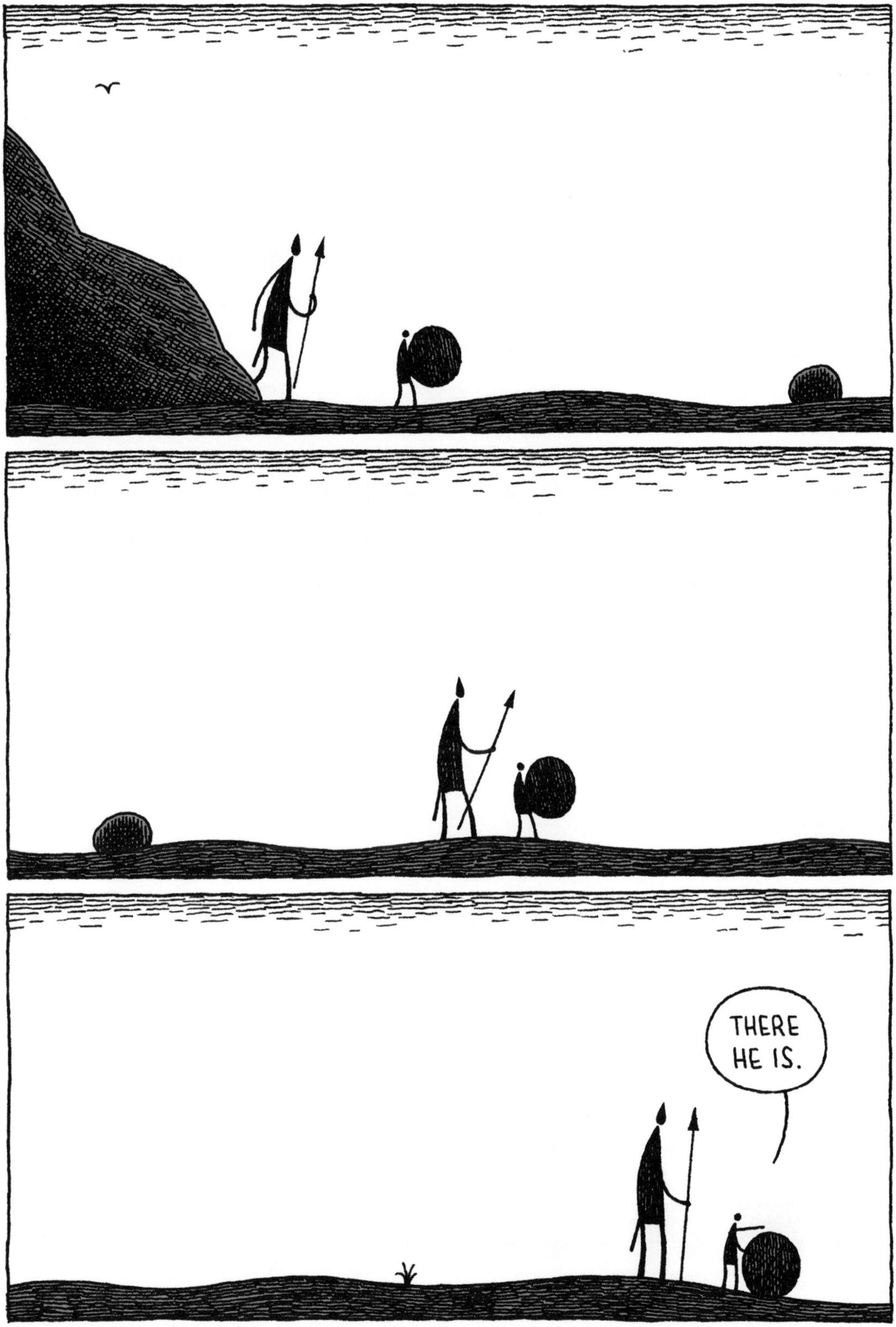
THERE HE IS.

GOOD
MORNING.
YOU'RE
BOTH WELL
I TRUST?

YES
SIR.

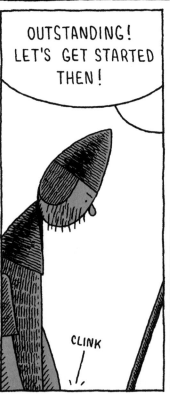

OUTSTANDING!
LET'S GET STARTED
THEN!

CLINK

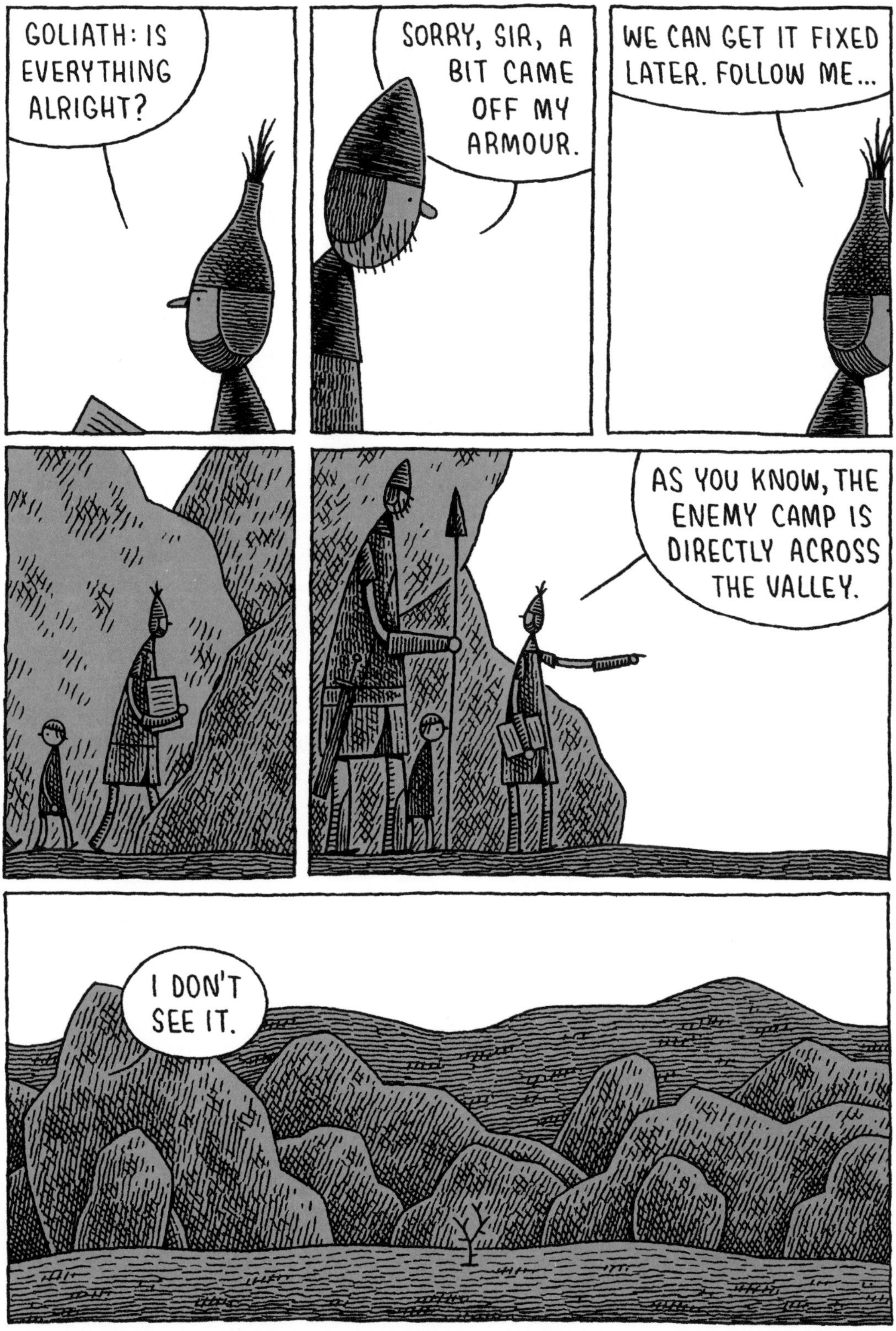
GOLIATH: IS EVERYTHING ALRIGHT?
SORRY, SIR, A BIT CAME OFF MY ARMOUR.
WE CAN GET IT FIXED LATER. FOLLOW ME...
AS YOU KNOW, THE ENEMY CAMP IS DIRECTLY ACROSS THE VALLEY.
I DON'T SEE IT.

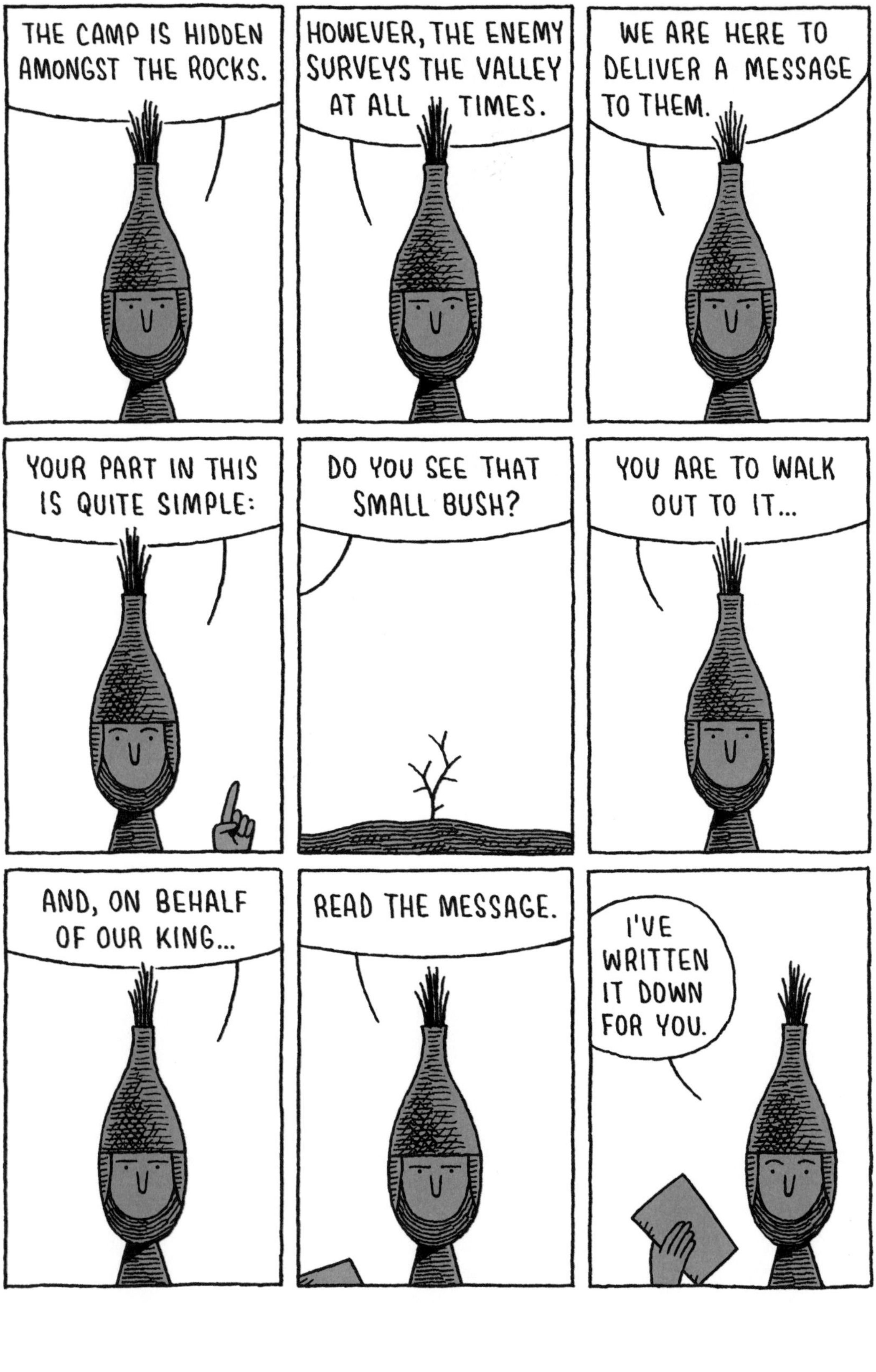
THE CAMP IS HIDDEN AMONGST THE ROCKS.
HOWEVER, THE ENEMY SURVEYS THE VALLEY AT ALL TIMES.
WE ARE HERE TO DELIVER A MESSAGE TO THEM.
YOUR PART IN THIS IS QUITE SIMPLE:
DO YOU SEE THAT SMALL BUSH?
YOU ARE TO WALK OUT TO IT...
AND, ON BEHALF OF OUR KING...
READ THE MESSAGE.
I'VE WRITTEN IT DOWN FOR YOU.

I AM GOLIATH OF GATH,
CHAMPION OF
THE PHILISTINES.

I CHALLENGE YOU:

CHOOSE A MAN,
LET HIM COME TO ME
THAT WE MAY FIGHT.

IF HE BE ABLE
TO KILL ME
THEN WE SHALL
BE YOUR SERVANTS.

BUT IF I KILL HIM
THEN YOU SHALL BE
OUR SERVANTS.

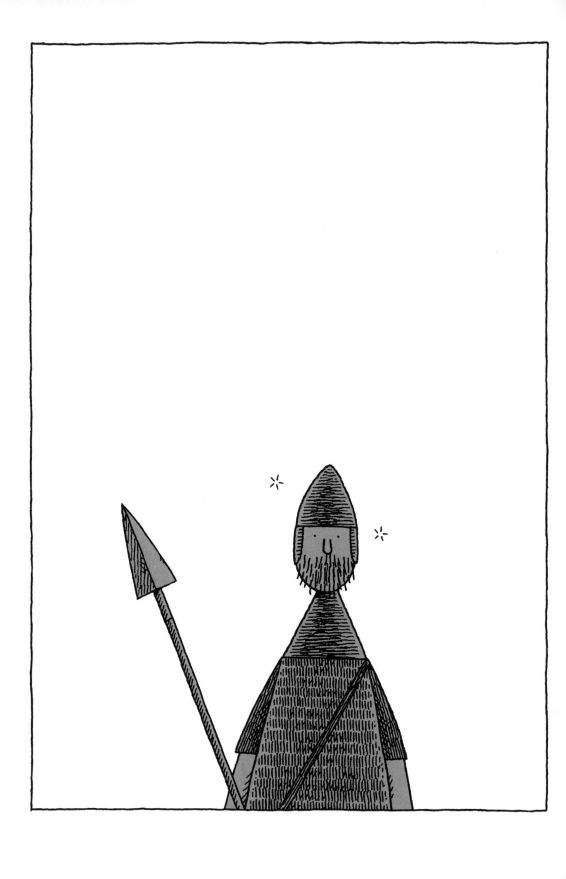

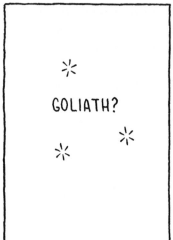

GOLIATH?

GOLIATH?

IS HE OK?

HE'LL BE FINE.

THERE'S BEEN A MISTAKE...

I'M NOT A CHAMPION. I'M THE FIFTH-WORST SWORDSMAN IN MY PLATOON...

...I DO PAPERWORK! I'M A VERY GOOD ADMINISTRATOR.

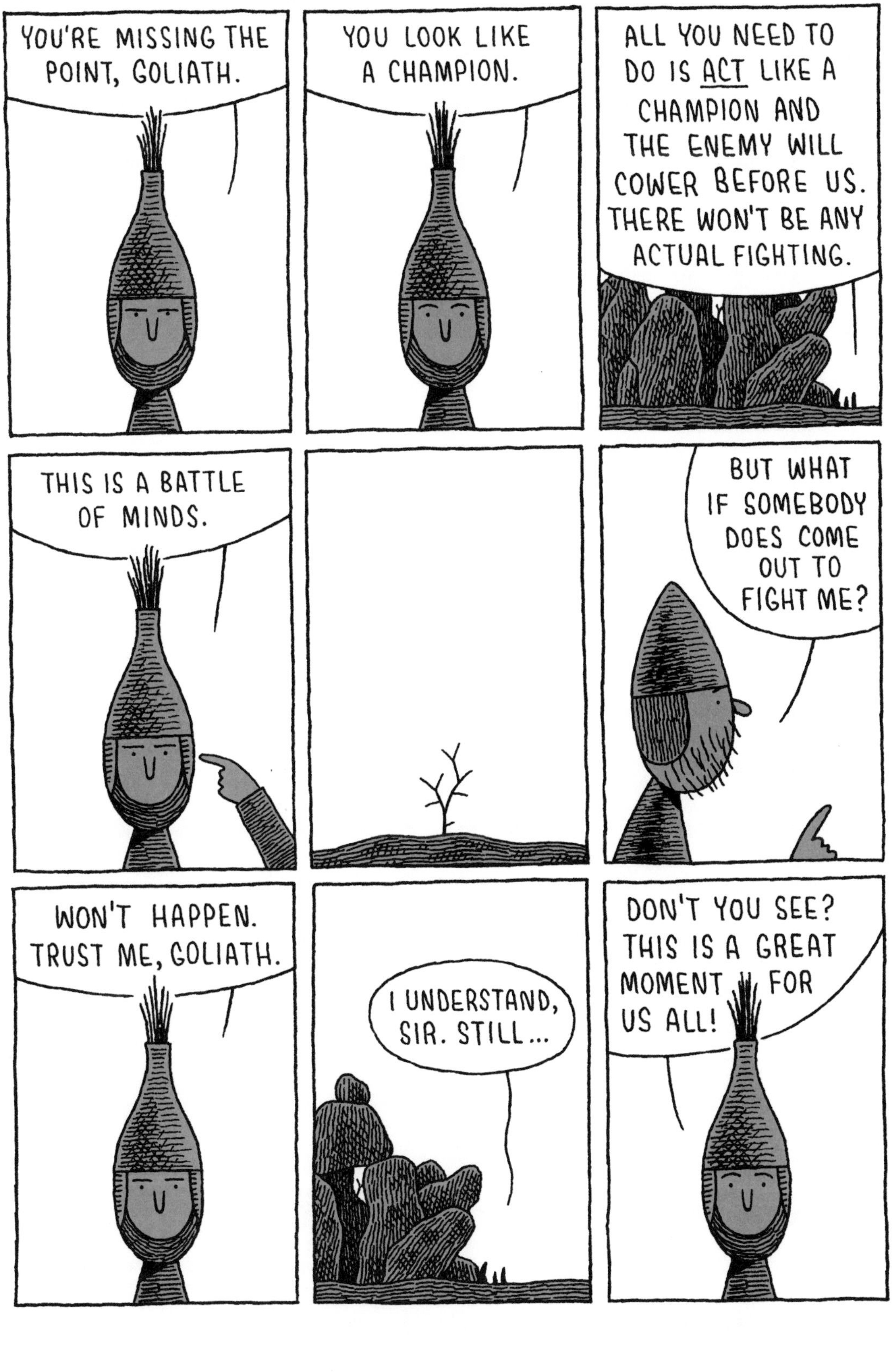
YOU'RE MISSING THE POINT, GOLIATH.
YOU LOOK LIKE A CHAMPION.
ALL YOU NEED TO DO IS ACT LIKE A CHAMPION AND THE ENEMY WILL COWER BEFORE US. THERE WON'T BE ANY ACTUAL FIGHTING.
THIS IS A BATTLE OF MINDS.
BUT WHAT IF SOMEBODY DOES COME OUT TO FIGHT ME?
WON'T HAPPEN. TRUST ME, GOLIATH.
I UNDERSTAND, SIR. STILL...
DON'T YOU SEE? THIS IS A GREAT MOMENT FOR US ALL!

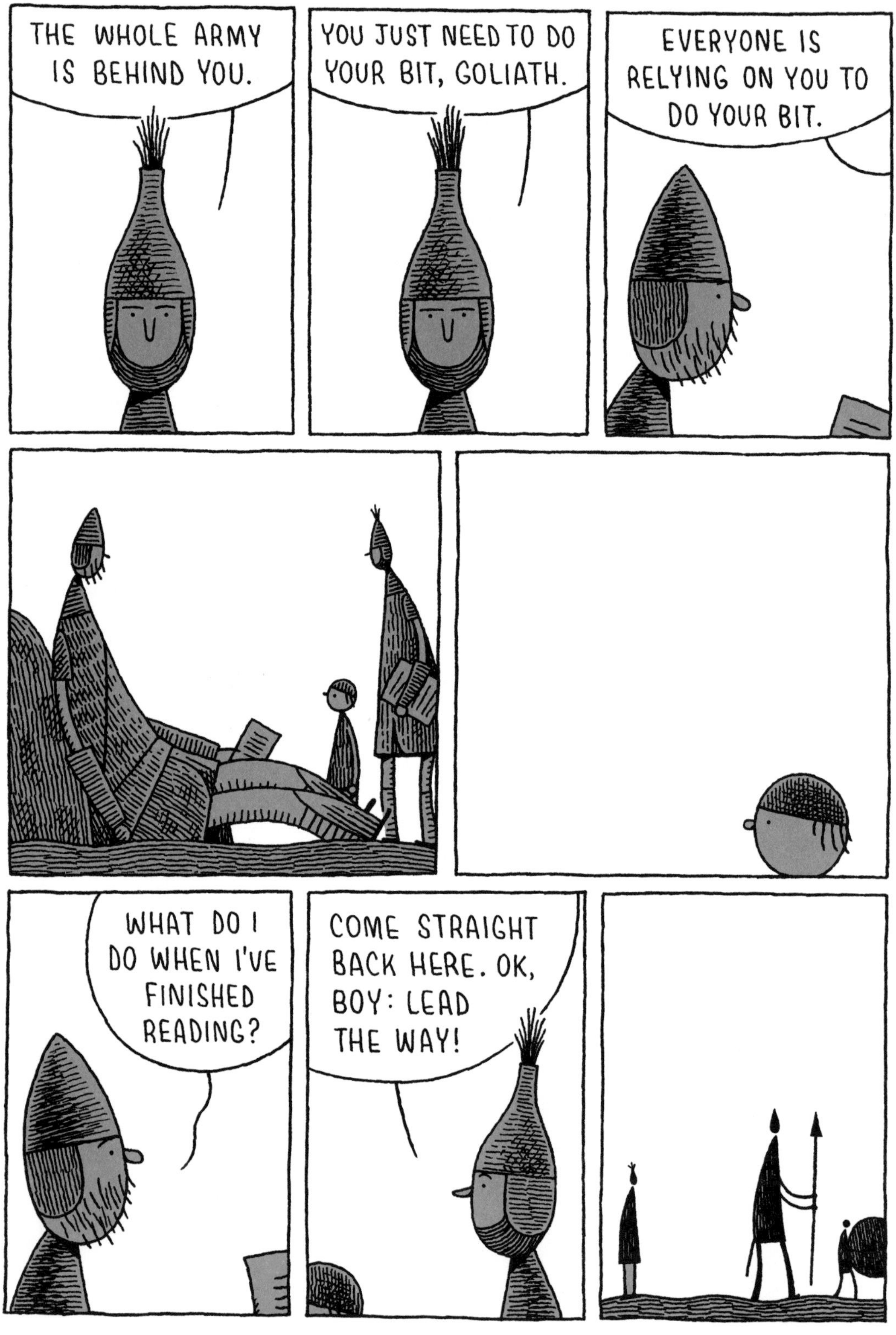
THE WHOLE ARMY IS BEHIND YOU.
YOU JUST NEED TO DO YOUR BIT, GOLIATH.
EVERYONE IS RELYING ON YOU TO DO YOUR BIT.
WHAT DO I DO WHEN I'VE FINISHED READING?
COME STRAIGHT BACK HERE. OK, BOY: LEAD THE WAY!

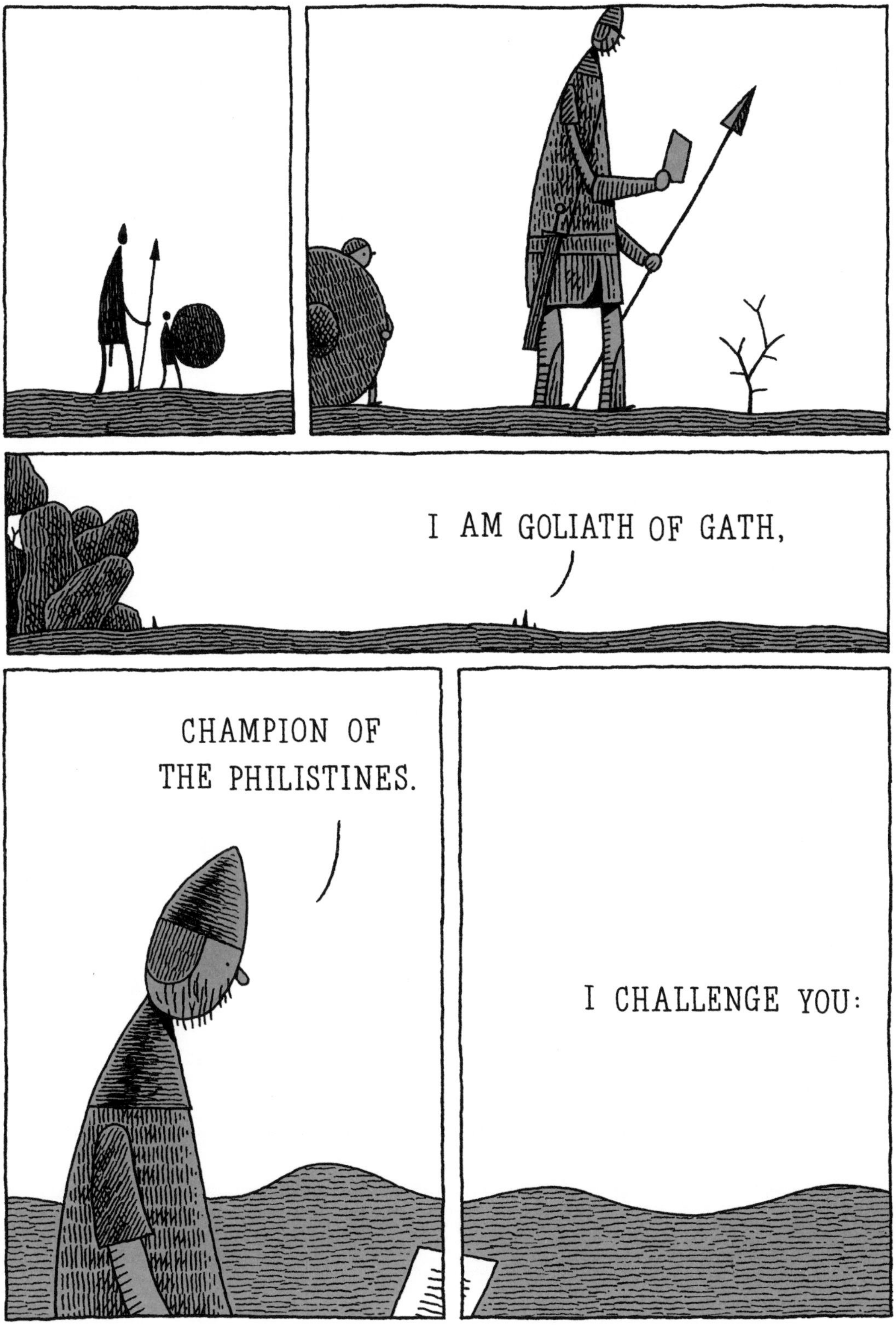
I AM GOLIATH OF GATH,
CHAMPION OF THE PHILISTINES.
I CHALLENGE YOU:

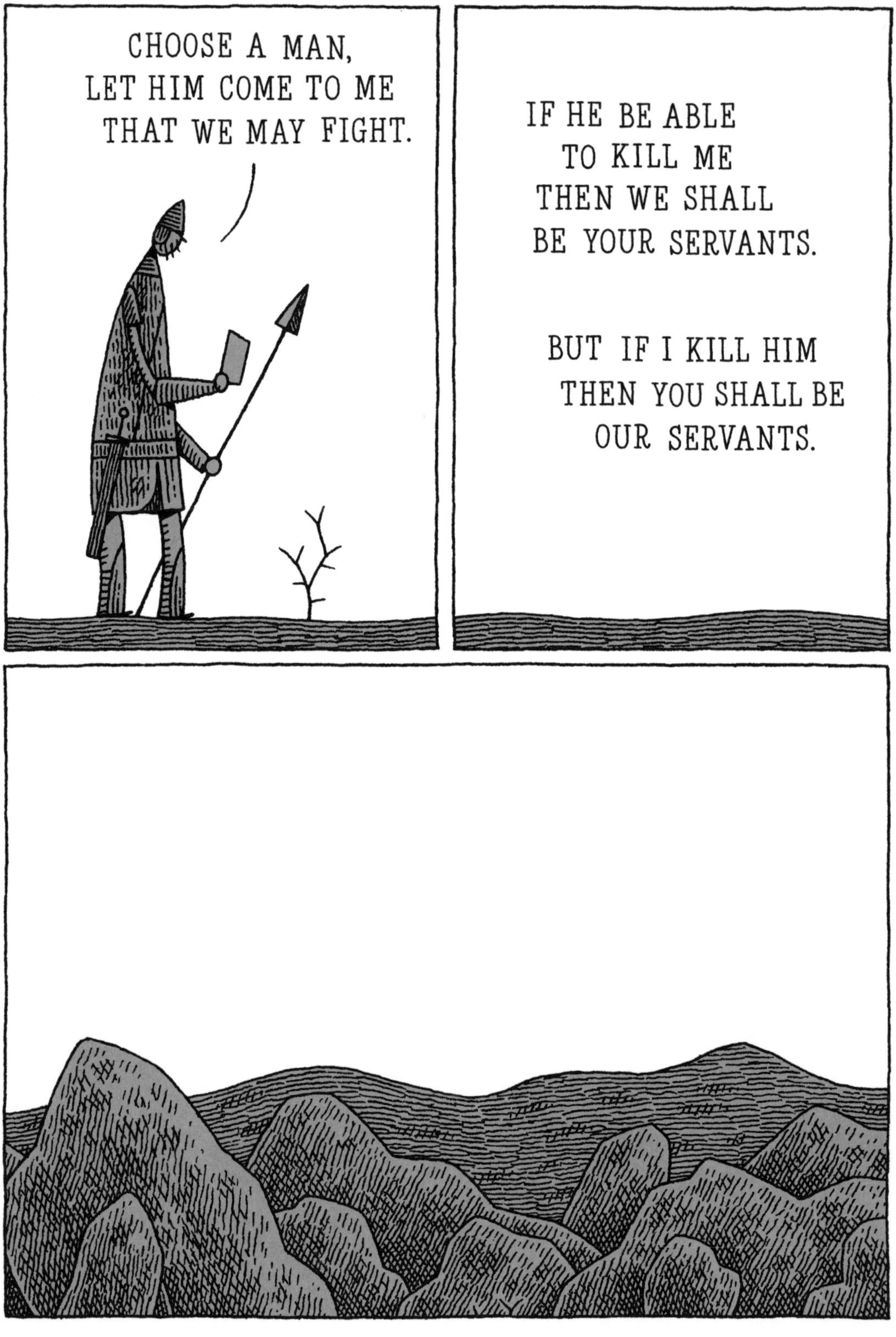
CHOOSE A MAN, LET HIM COME TO ME THAT WE MAY FIGHT.
IF HE BE ABLE TO KILL ME THEN WE SHALL BE YOUR SERVANTS.
BUT IF I KILL HIM THEN YOU SHALL BE OUR SERVANTS.

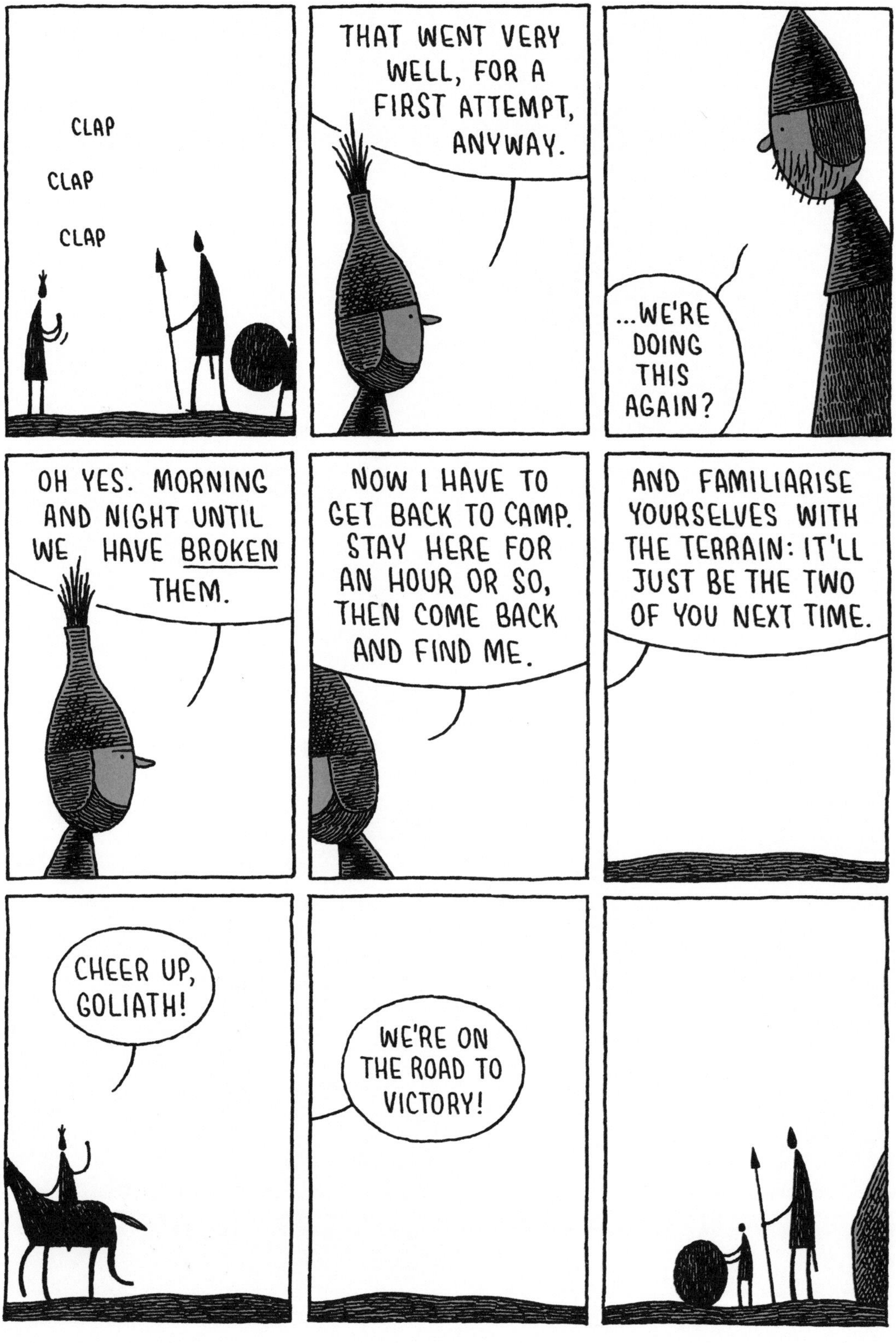
CLAP
CLAP
CLAP
THAT WENT VERY WELL, FOR A FIRST ATTEMPT, ANYWAY.
...WE'RE DOING THIS AGAIN?
OH YES. MORNING AND NIGHT UNTIL WE HAVE BROKEN THEM.
NOW I HAVE TO GET BACK TO CAMP. STAY HERE FOR AN HOUR OR SO, THEN COME BACK AND FIND ME.
AND FAMILIARISE YOURSELVES WITH THE TERRAIN: IT'LL JUST BE THE TWO OF YOU NEXT TIME.
CHEER UP, GOLIATH!
WE'RE ON THE ROAD TO VICTORY!

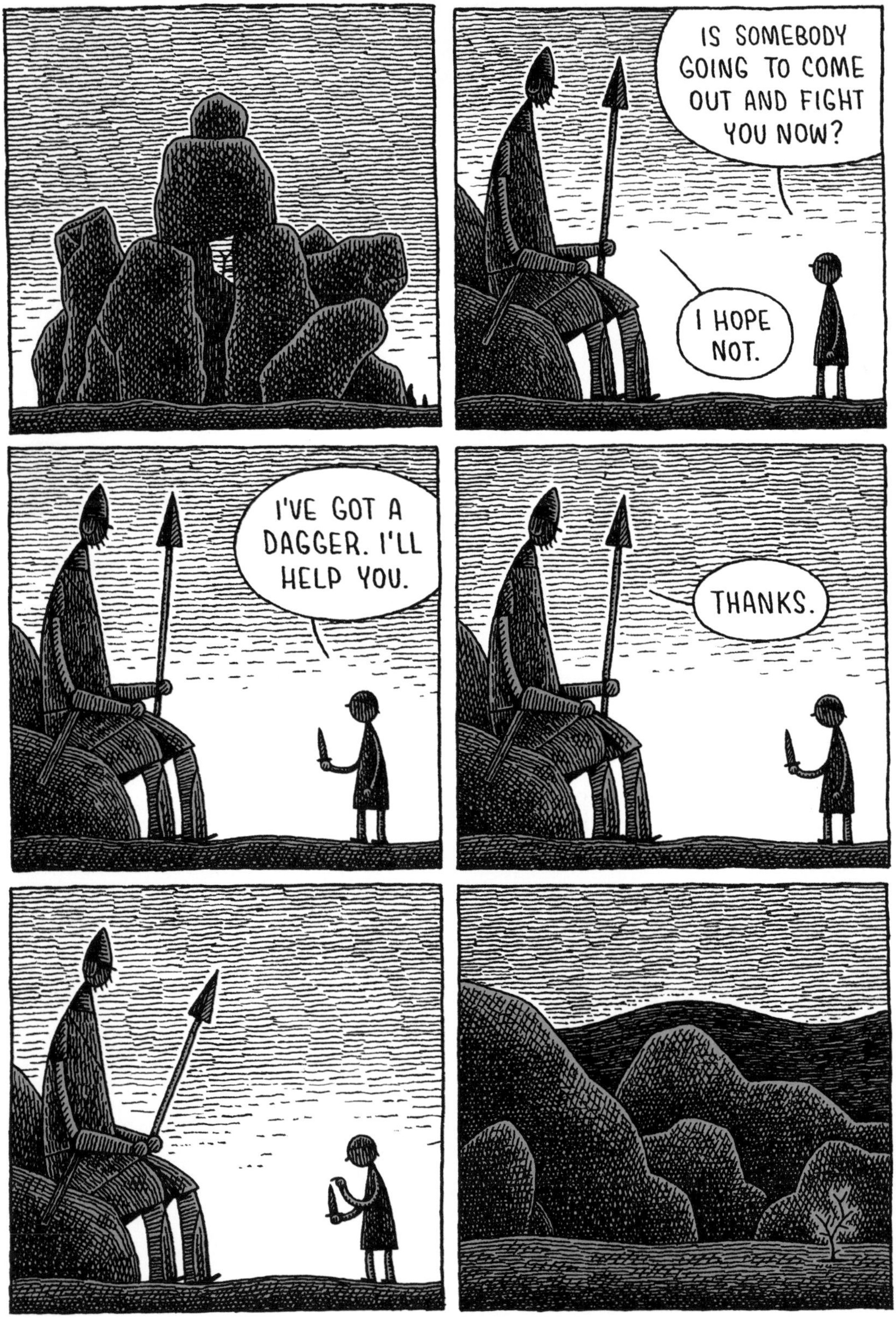

IS SOMEBODY GOING TO COME OUT AND FIGHT YOU NOW?
I HOPE NOT.
I'VE GOT A DAGGER. I'LL HELP YOU.
THANKS.

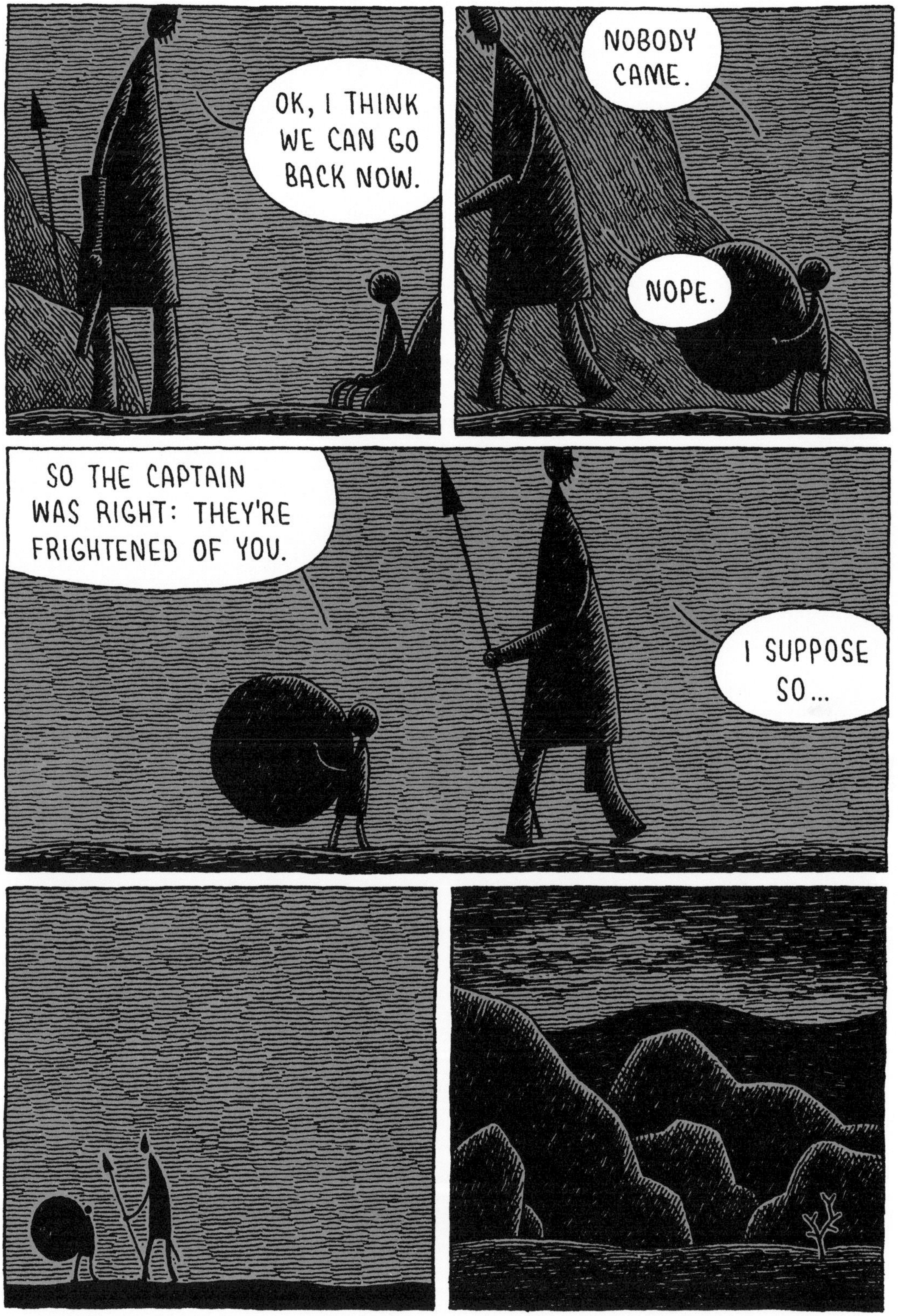
OK, I THINK WE CAN GO BACK NOW.
NOBODY CAME.
NOPE.
SO THE CAPTAIN WAS RIGHT: THEY'RE FRIGHTENED OF YOU.
I SUPPOSE SO...

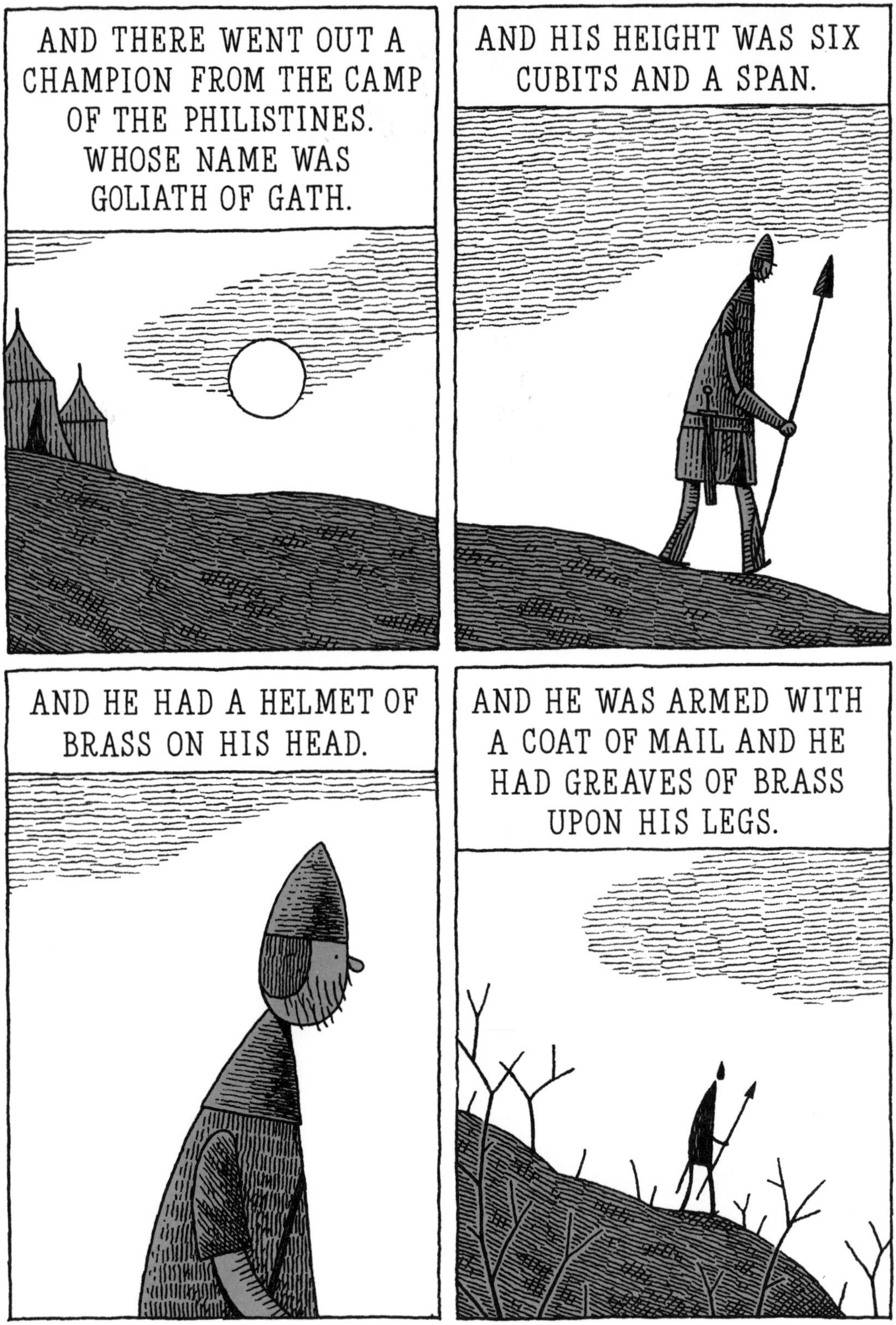
AND THERE WENT OUT A CHAMPION FROM THE CAMP OF THE PHILISTINES. WHOSE NAME WAS GOLIATH OF GATH.
AND HIS HEIGHT WAS SIX CUBITS AND A SPAN.
AND HE HAD A HELMET OF BRASS ON HIS HEAD.
AND HE WAS ARMED WITH A COAT OF MAIL AND HE HAD GREAVES OF BRASS UPON HIS LEGS.

AND THE STAFF OF HIS
SPEAR WAS LIKE A
WEAVER'S BEAM;
AND HIS SPEAR'S HEAD
WEIGHED SIX HUNDRED
SHEKELS OF IRON.

AND ONE BEARING A
SHIELD WENT BEFORE HIM.

AND THE PHILISTINE
DREW NEAR EACH
MORNING AND NIGHT
AND PRESENTED HIMSELF TO
THE ARMIES OF ISRAEL.

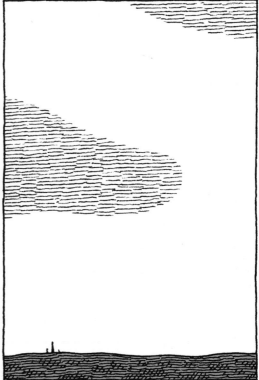

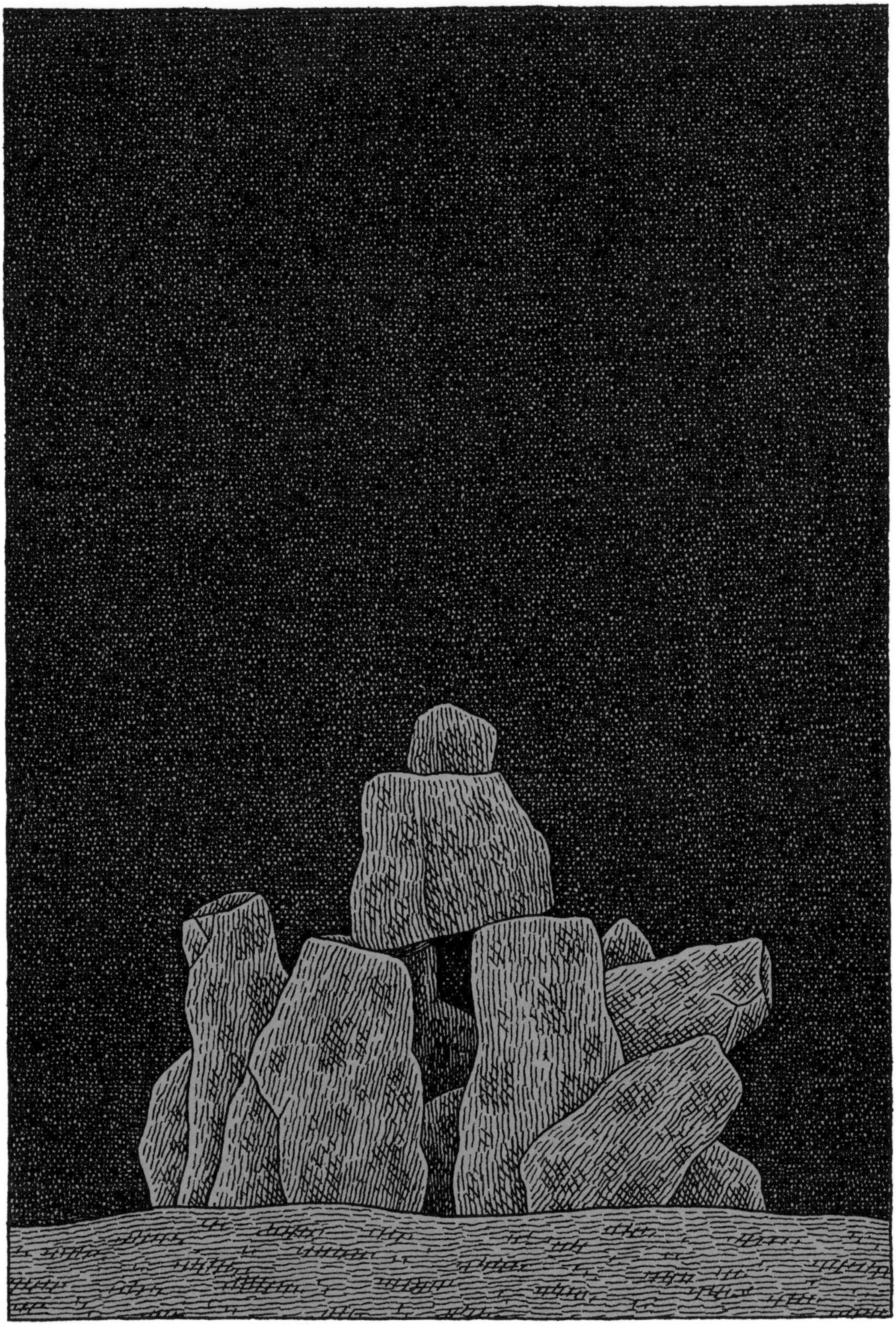

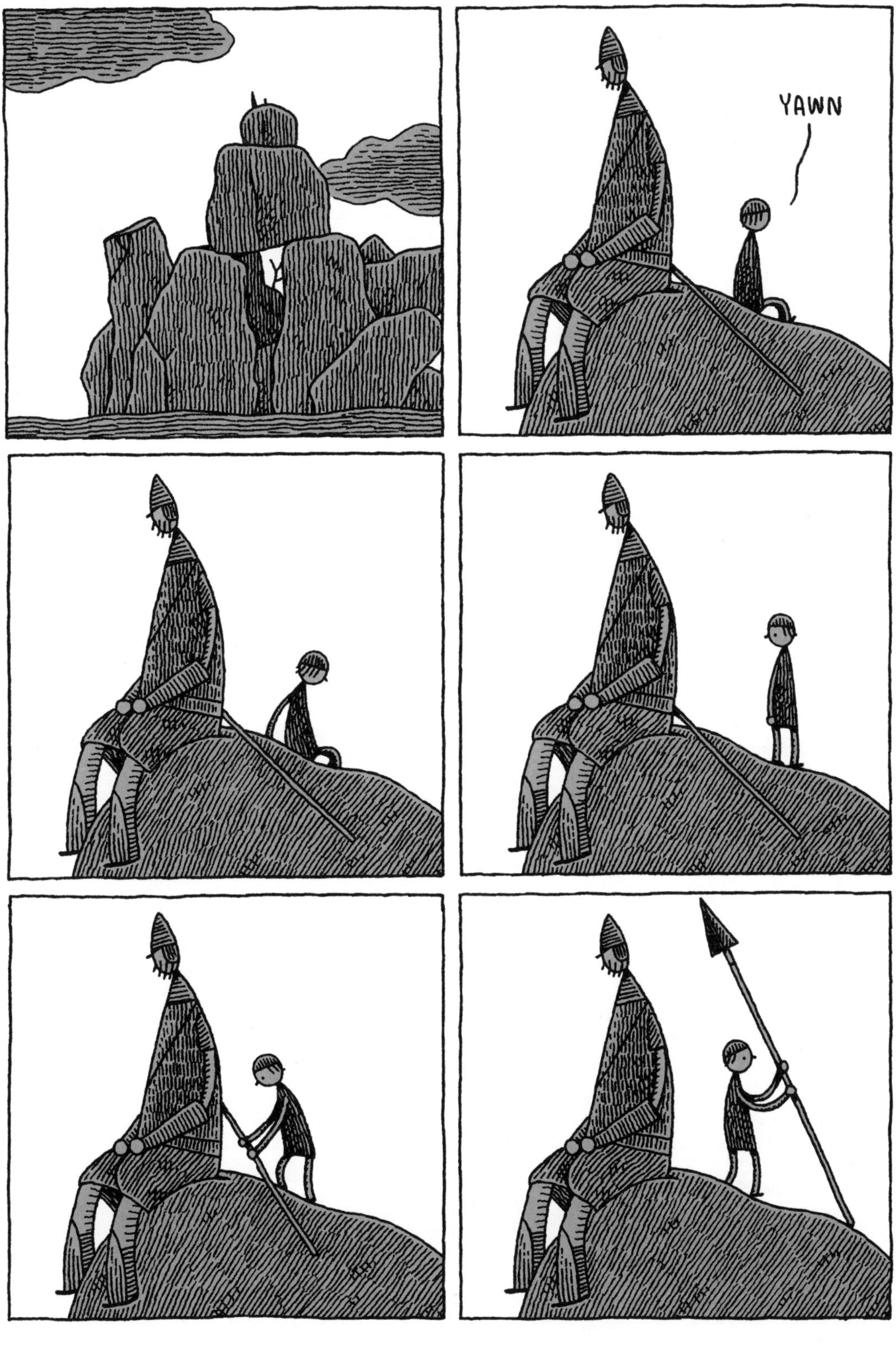
YAWN

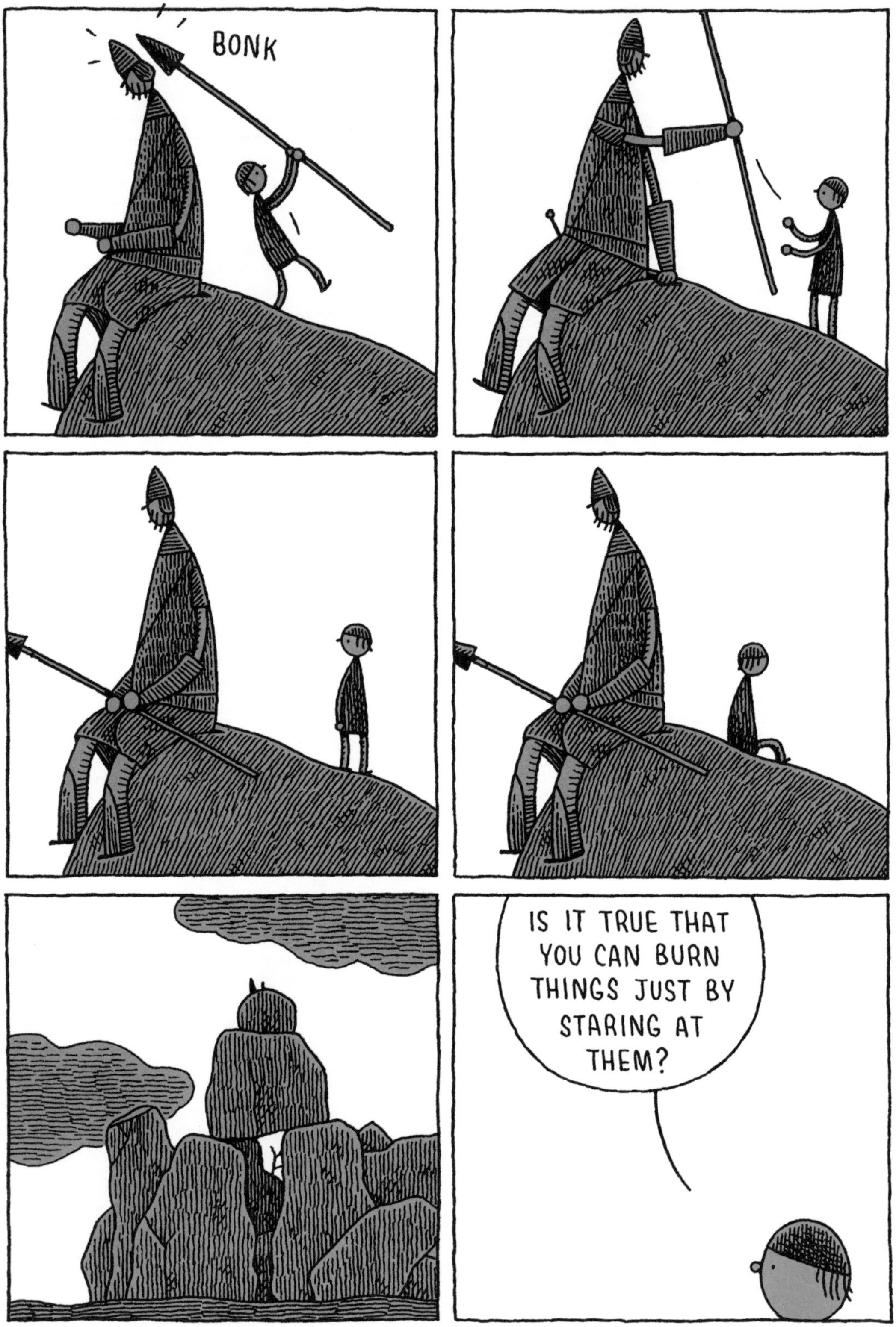
BONK
IS IT TRUE THAT YOU CAN BURN THINGS JUST BY STARING AT THEM?

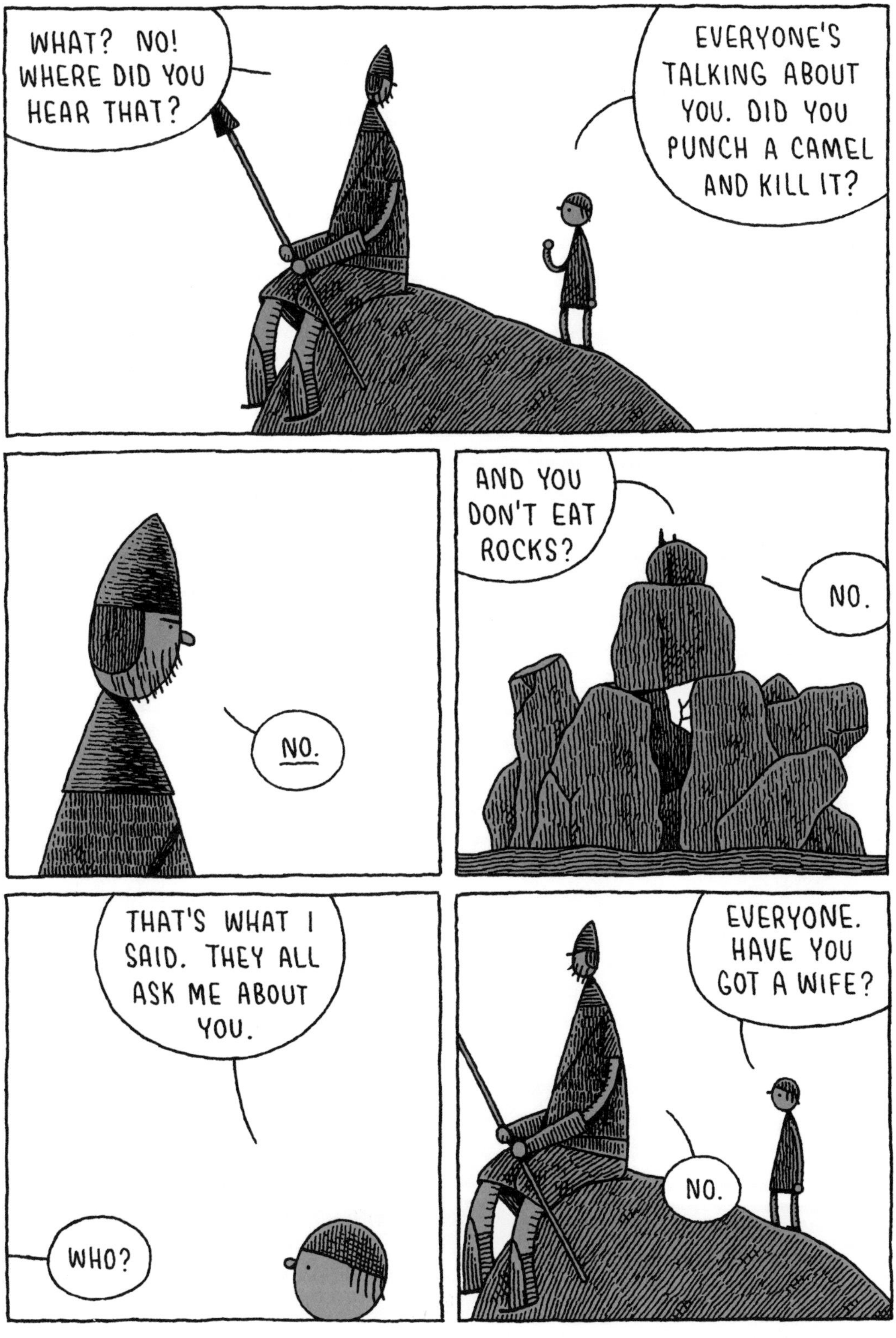
EVERYONE'S TALKING ABOUT YOU. DID YOU PUNCH A CAMEL AND KILL IT?
WHAT? NO! WHERE DID YOU HEAR THAT?
NO.
AND YOU DON'T EAT ROCKS?
NO.
THAT'S WHAT I SAID. THEY ALL ASK ME ABOUT YOU.
WHO?
EVERYONE. HAVE YOU GOT A WIFE?
NO.

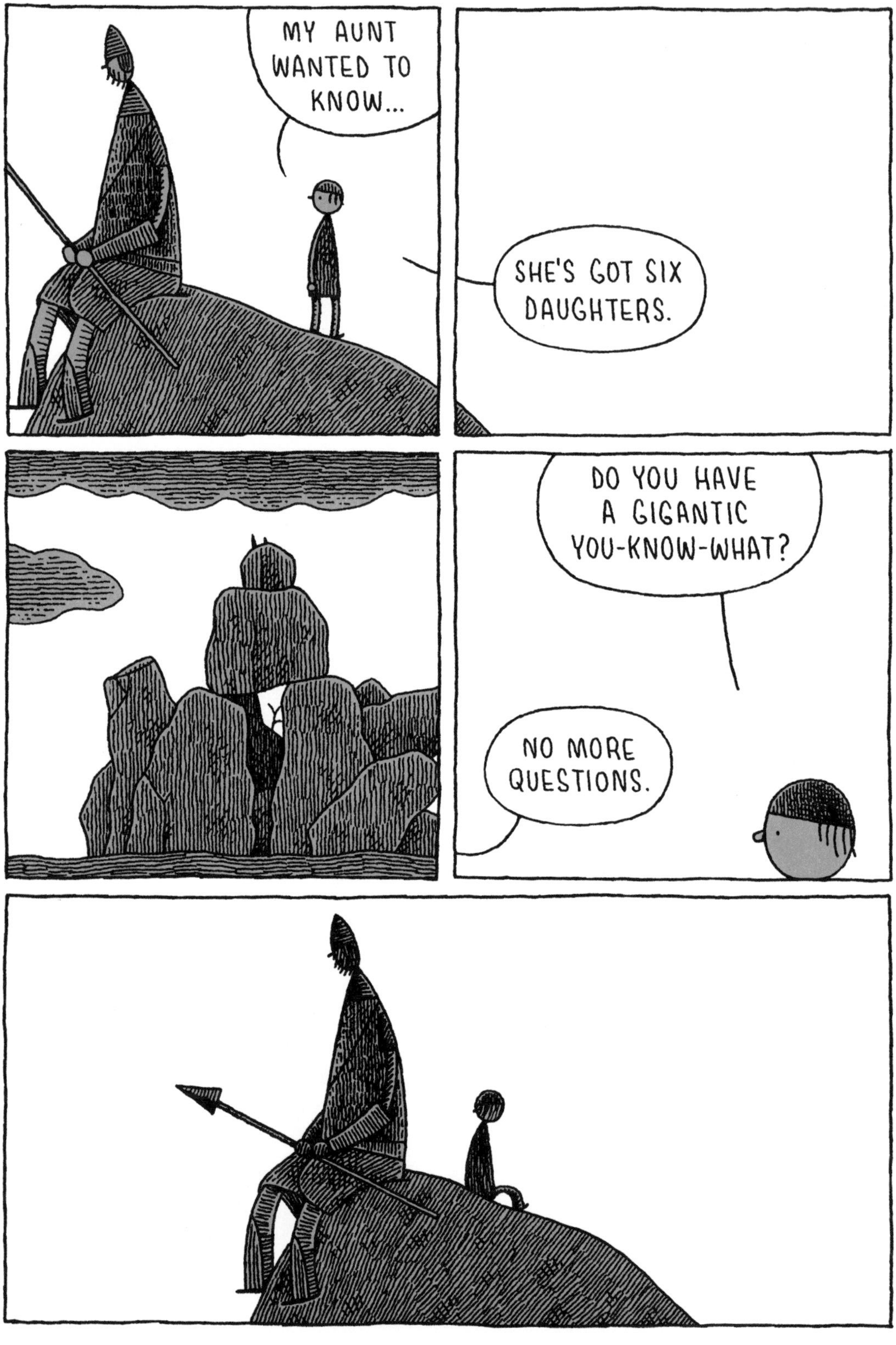
MY AUNT WANTED TO KNOW...
SHE'S GOT SIX DAUGHTERS.
DO YOU HAVE A GIGANTIC YOU-KNOW-WHAT?
NO MORE QUESTIONS.

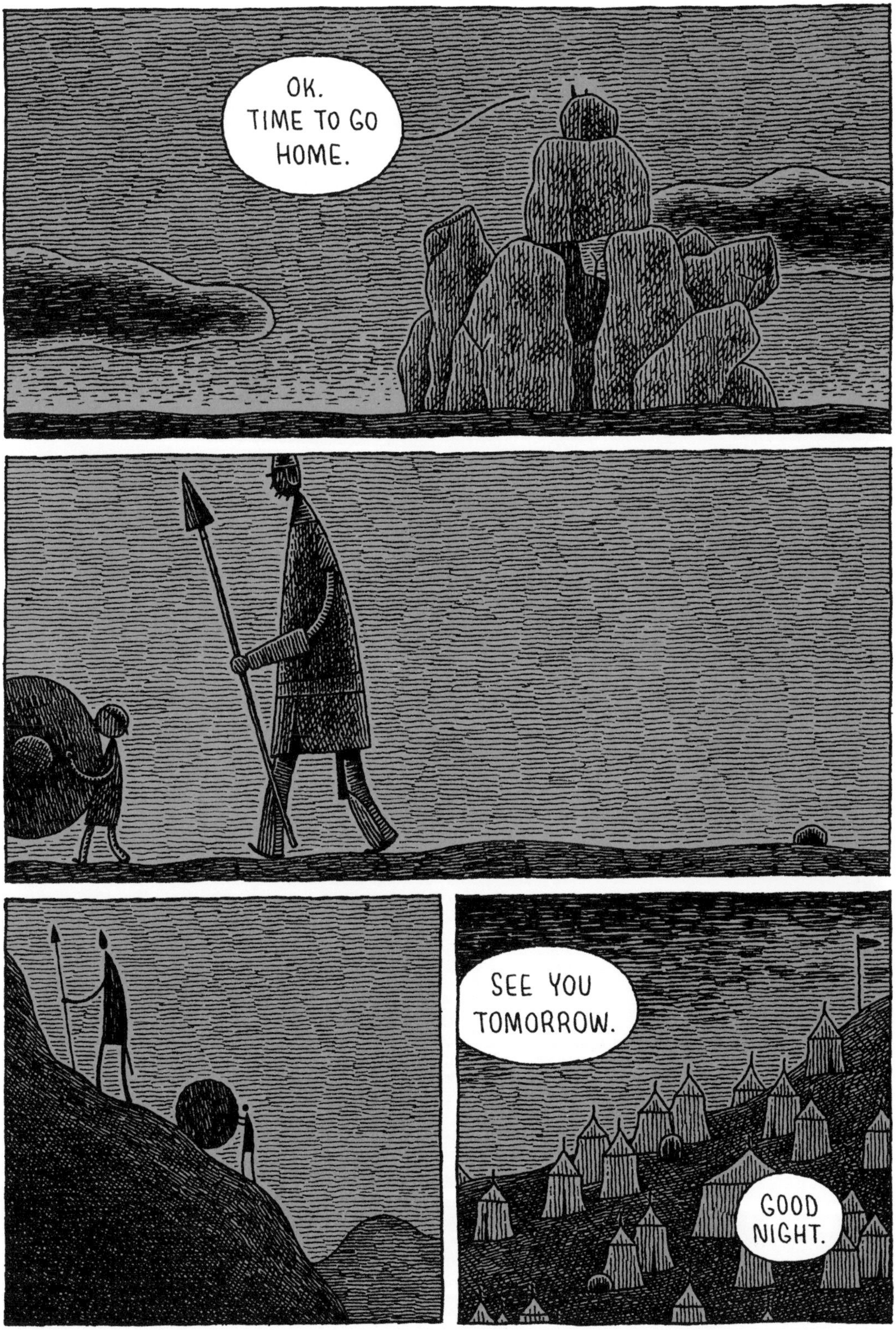
OK. TIME TO GO HOME.
SEE YOU TOMORROW.
GOOD NIGHT.

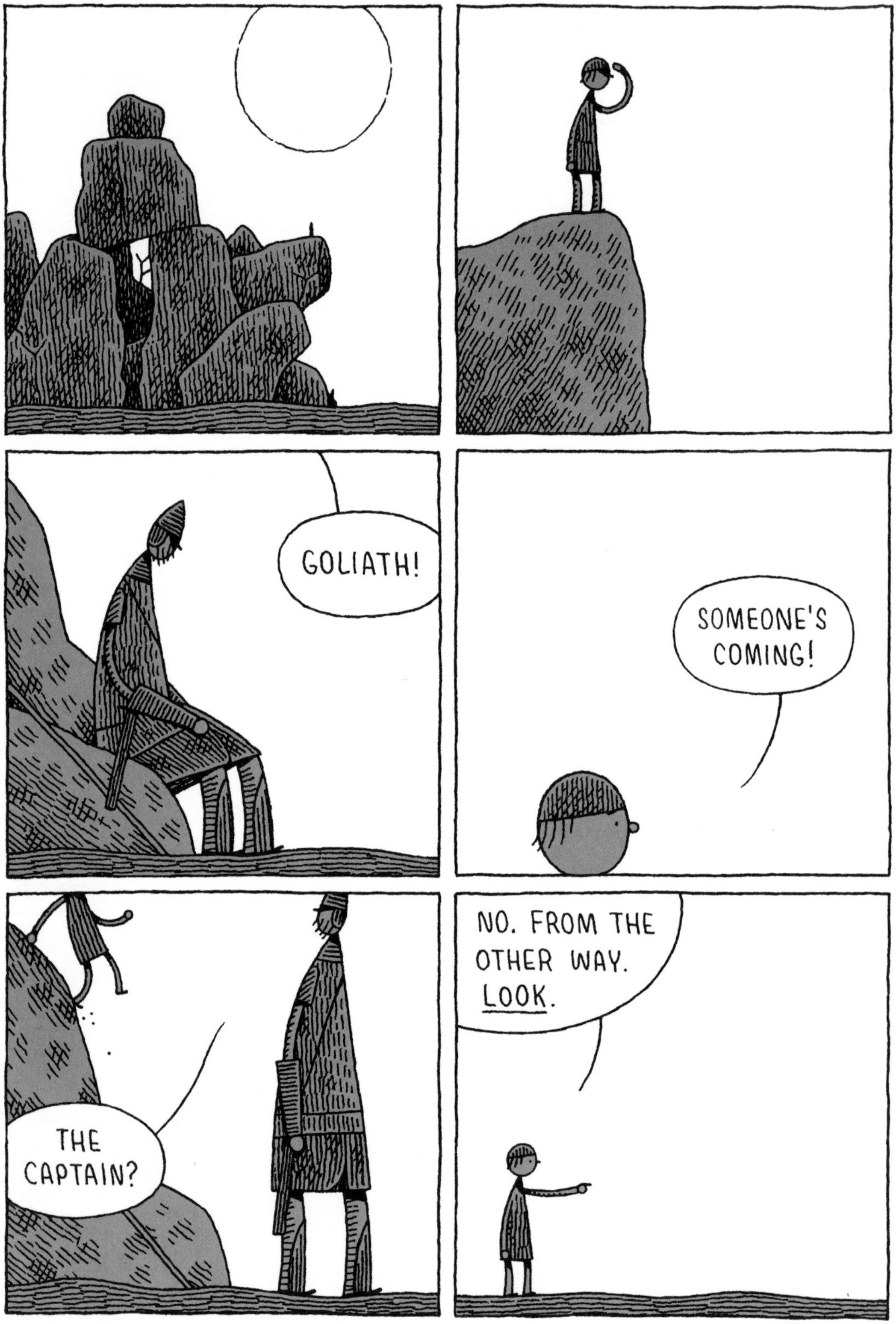
GOLIATH!
SOMEONE'S COMING!
THE CAPTAIN?
NO. FROM THE OTHER WAY. LOOK.

YOU SHOULD GO.

WHAT?

RUN AWAY.

WHERE?

HIDE IN THE ROCKS.

I'LL STAY. I'LL HELP.

NO. GO AWAY.

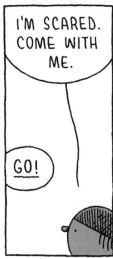

I'M SCARED. COME WITH ME.

GO!

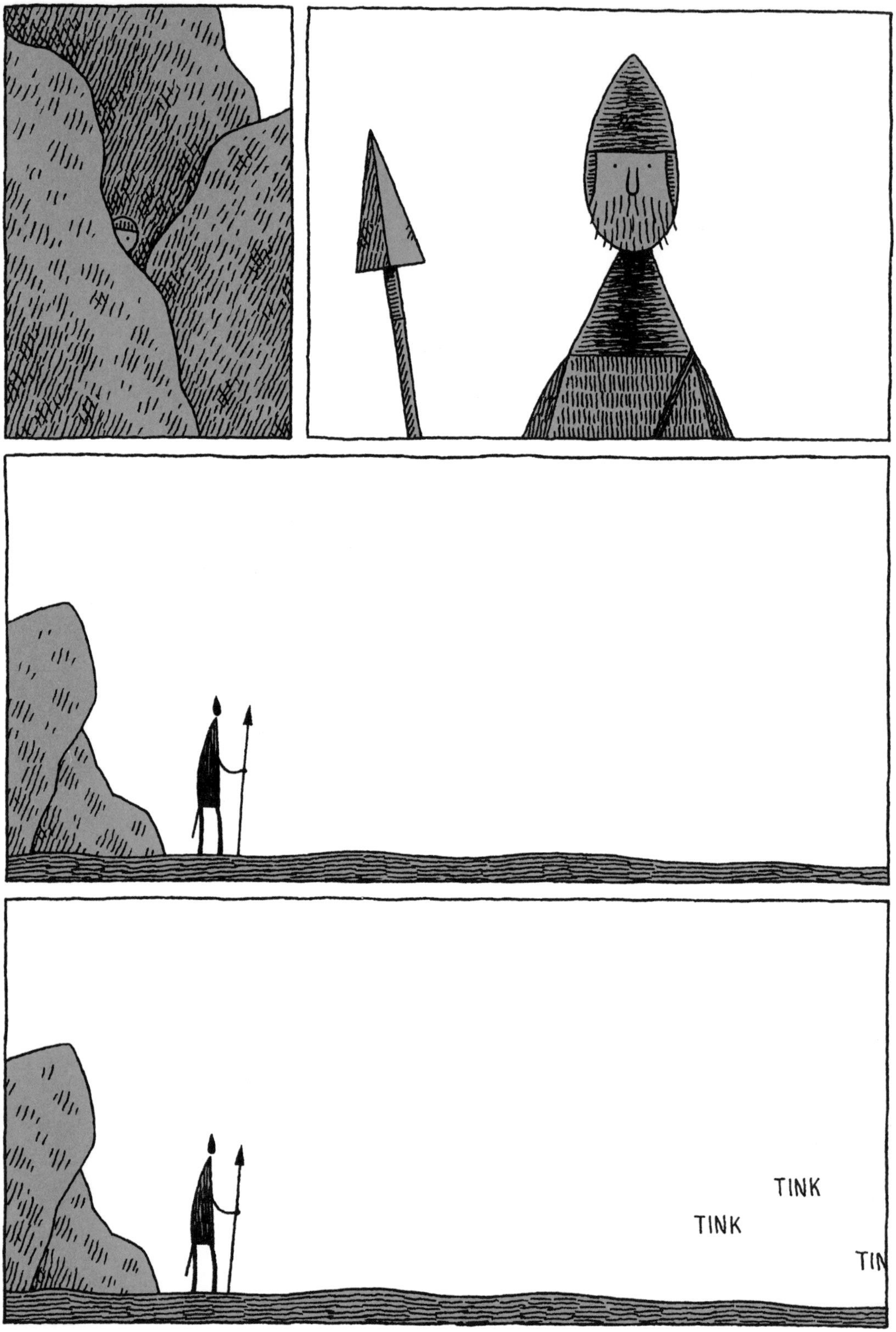
TINK
TINK
TIN

TINK

TINK

TINK

WHAT?

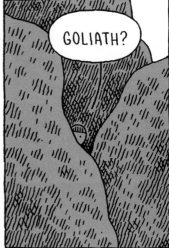

GOLIATH?

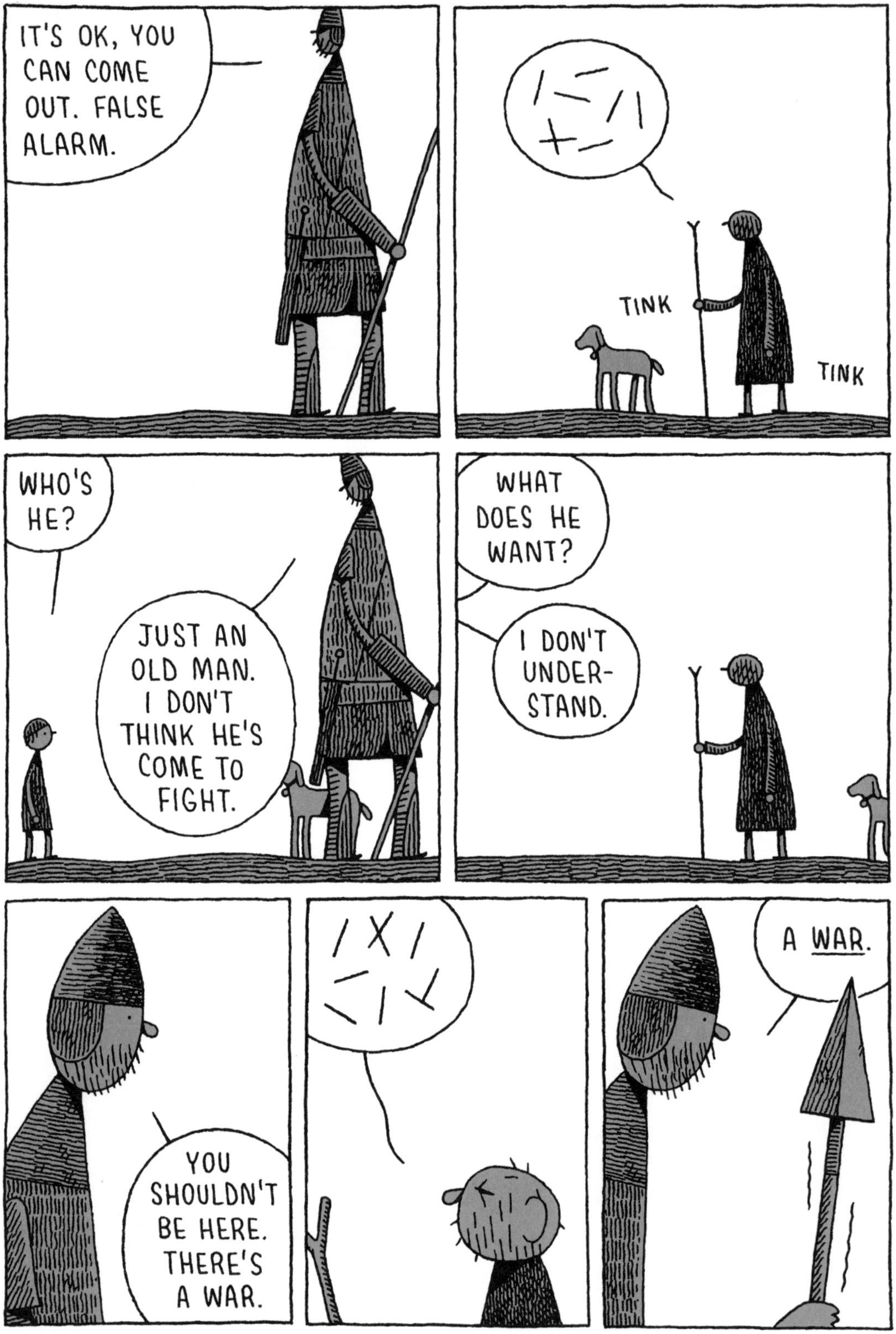
IT'S OK, YOU CAN COME OUT. FALSE ALARM.
TINK
TINK
WHO'S HE?
JUST AN OLD MAN. I DON'T THINK HE'S COME TO FIGHT.
WHAT DOES HE WANT?
I DON'T UNDER-STAND.
YOU SHOULDN'T BE HERE. THERE'S A WAR.
A WAR.

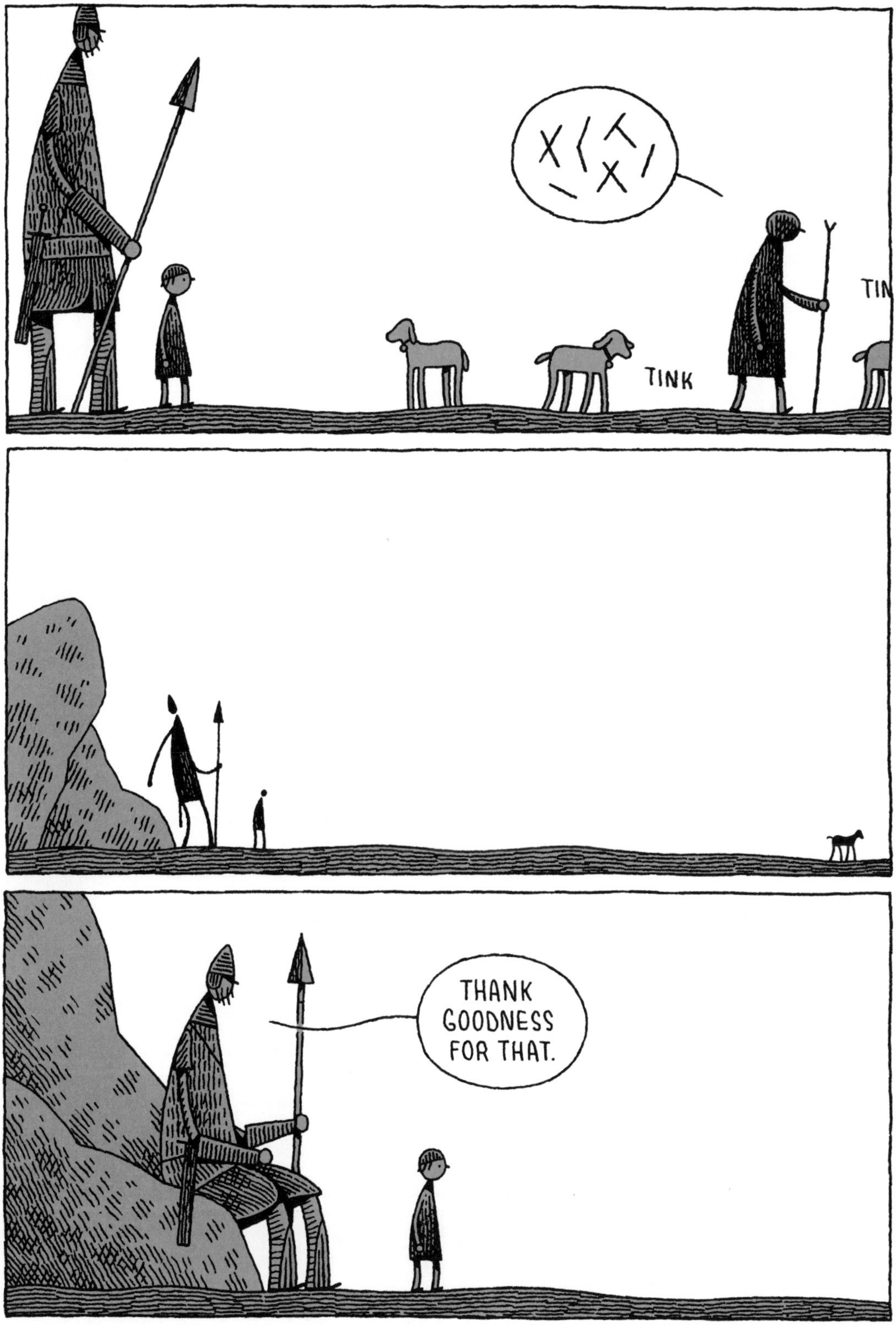
TIN
TINK
THANK GOODNESS FOR THAT.

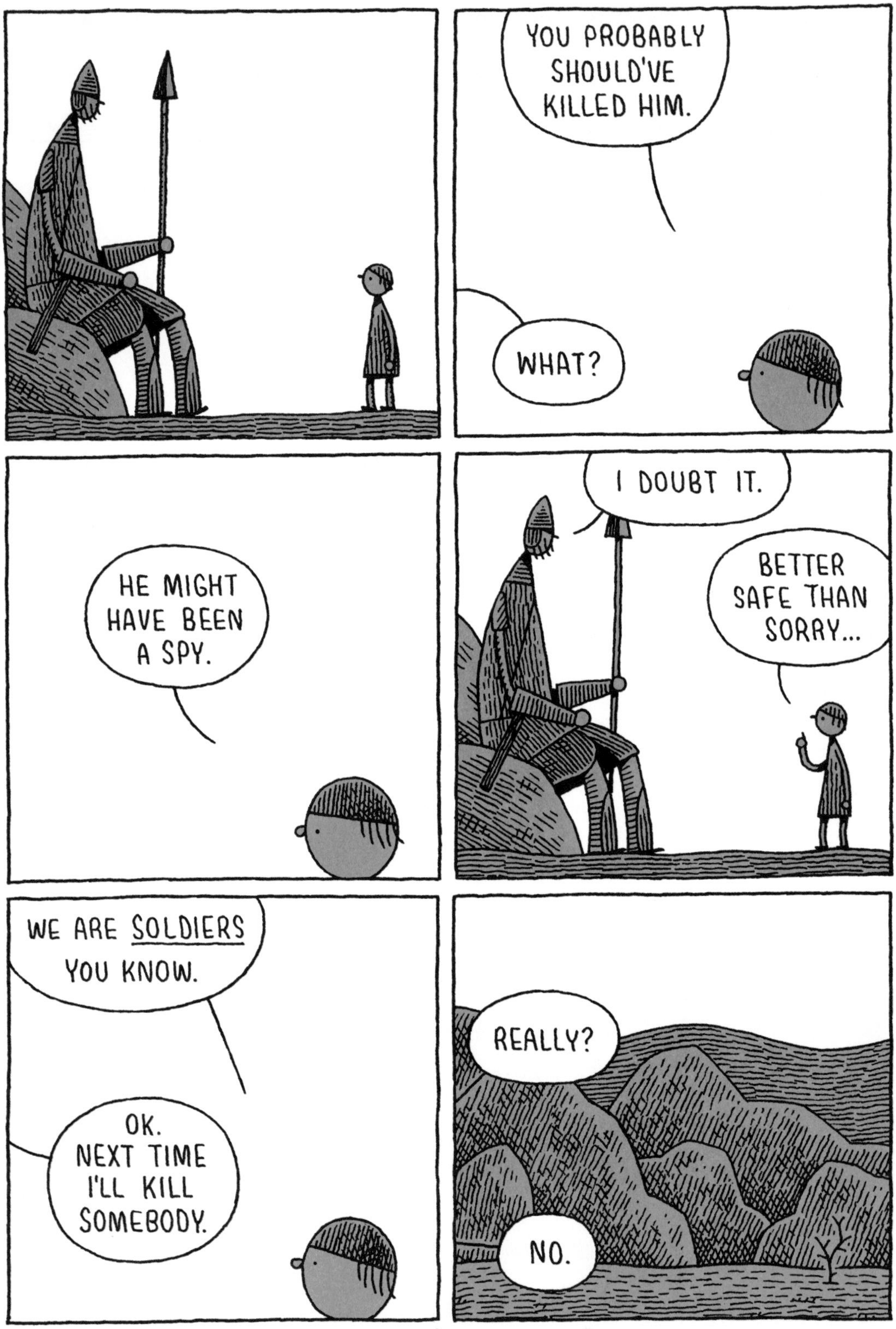
YOU PROBABLY SHOULD'VE KILLED HIM.
WHAT?
HE MIGHT HAVE BEEN A SPY.
I DOUBT IT.
BETTER SAFE THAN SORRY...
WE ARE SOLDIERS YOU KNOW.
OK. NEXT TIME I'LL KILL SOMEBODY.
REALLY?
NO.

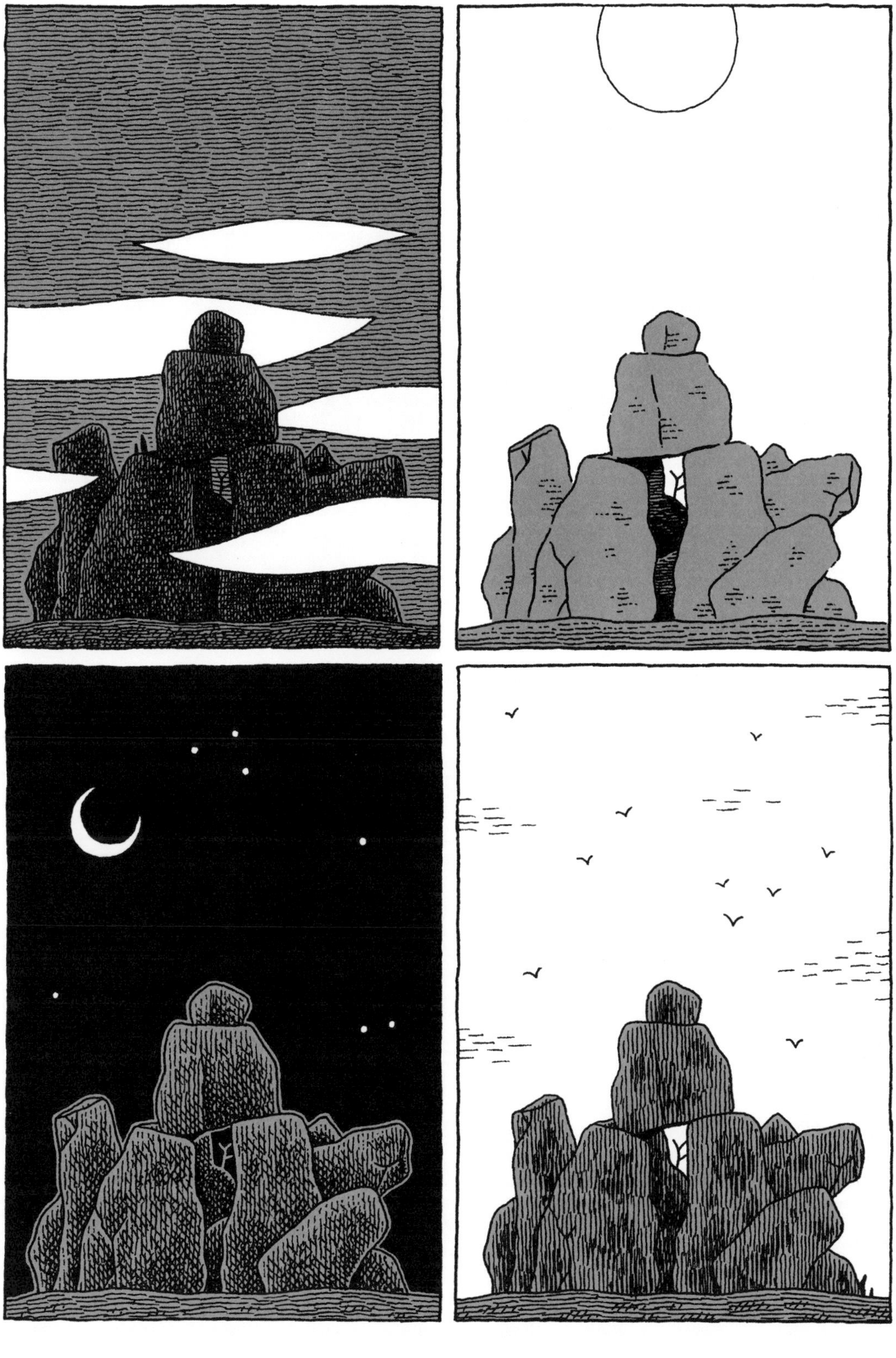

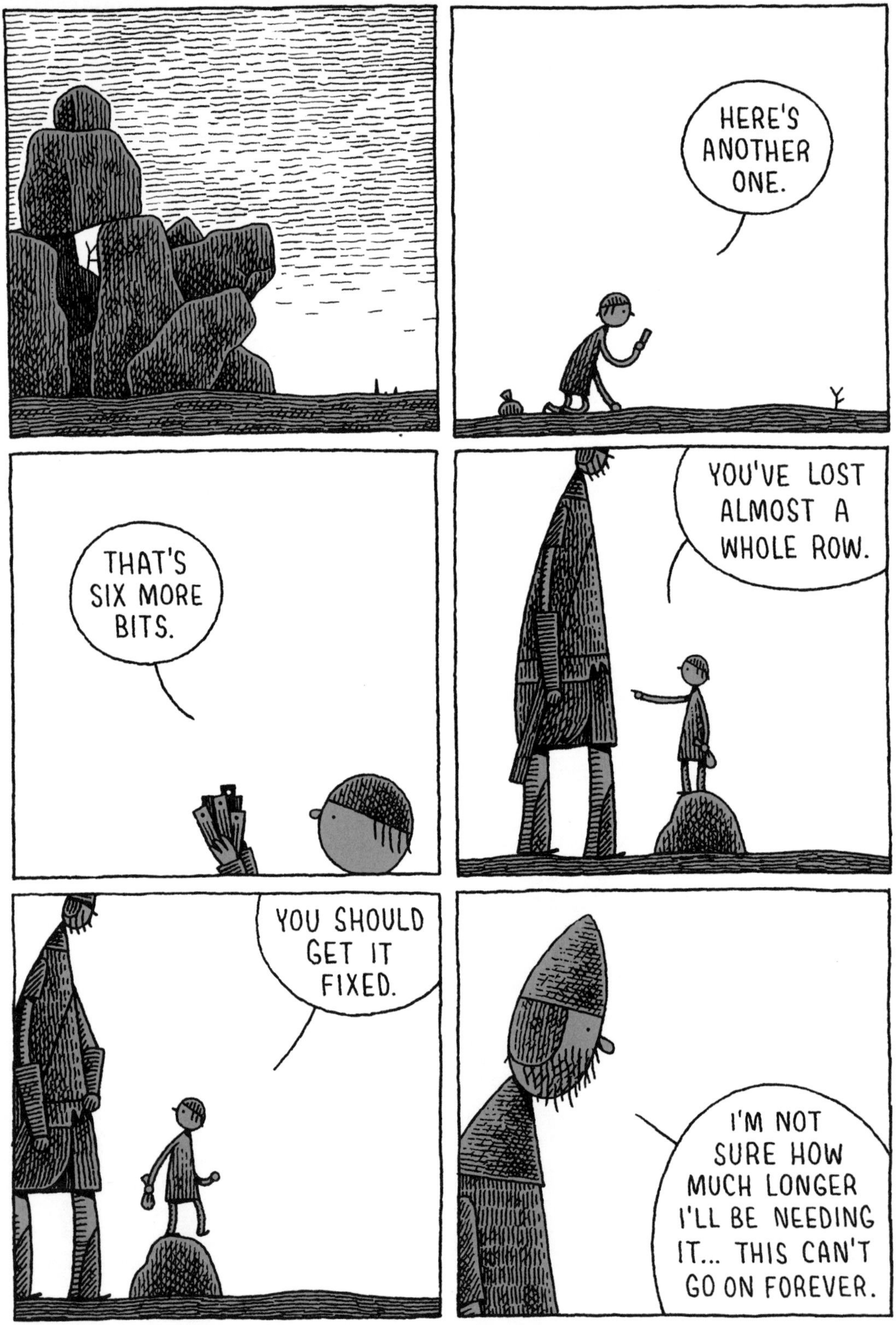
HERE'S ANOTHER ONE.
THAT'S SIX MORE BITS.
YOU'VE LOST ALMOST A WHOLE ROW.
YOU SHOULD GET IT FIXED.
I'M NOT SURE HOW MUCH LONGER I'LL BE NEEDING IT... THIS CAN'T GO ON FOREVER.

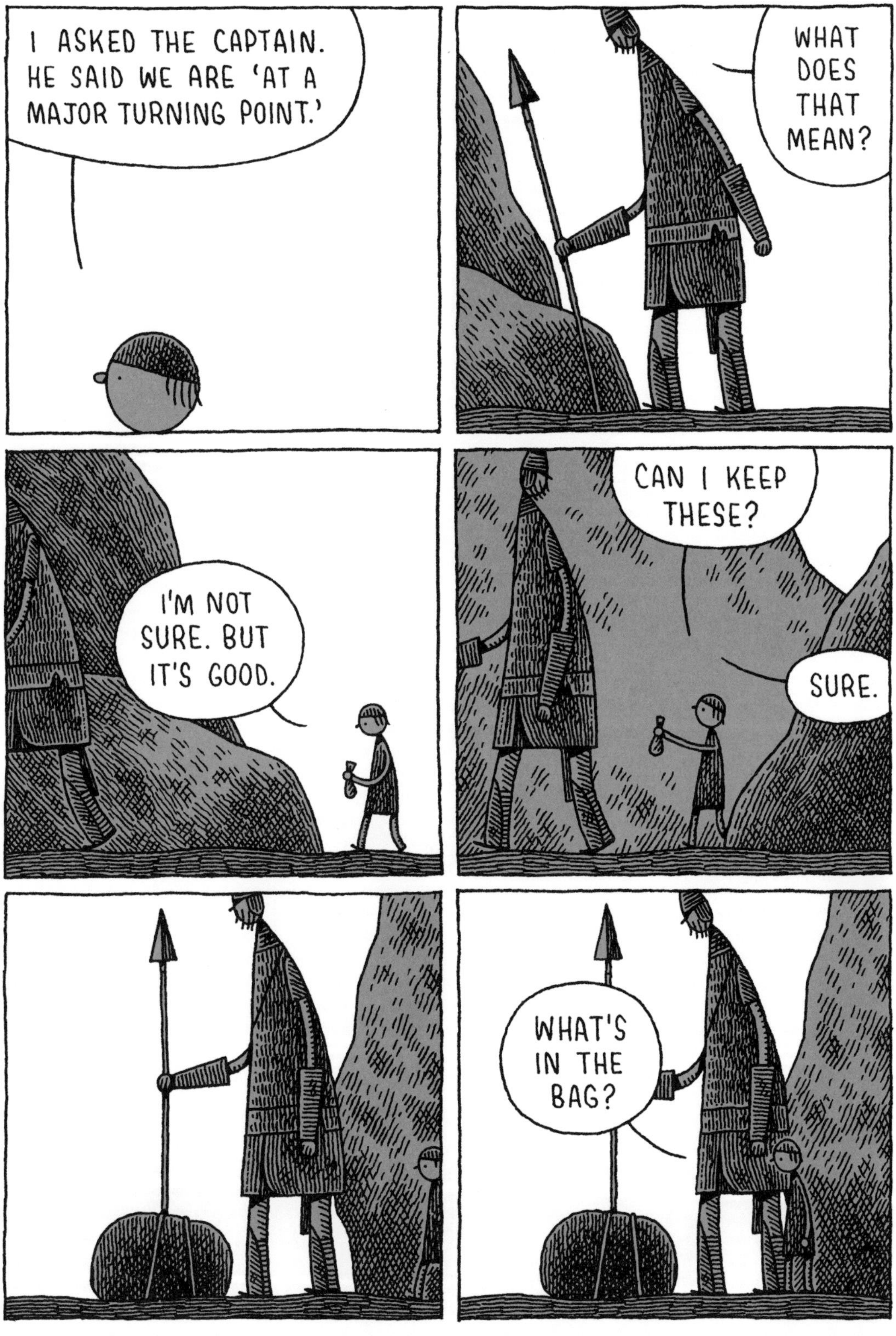
I ASKED THE CAPTAIN. HE SAID WE ARE 'AT A MAJOR TURNING POINT.'
WHAT DOES THAT MEAN?
I'M NOT SURE. BUT IT'S GOOD.
CAN I KEEP THESE?
SURE.
WHAT'S IN THE BAG?

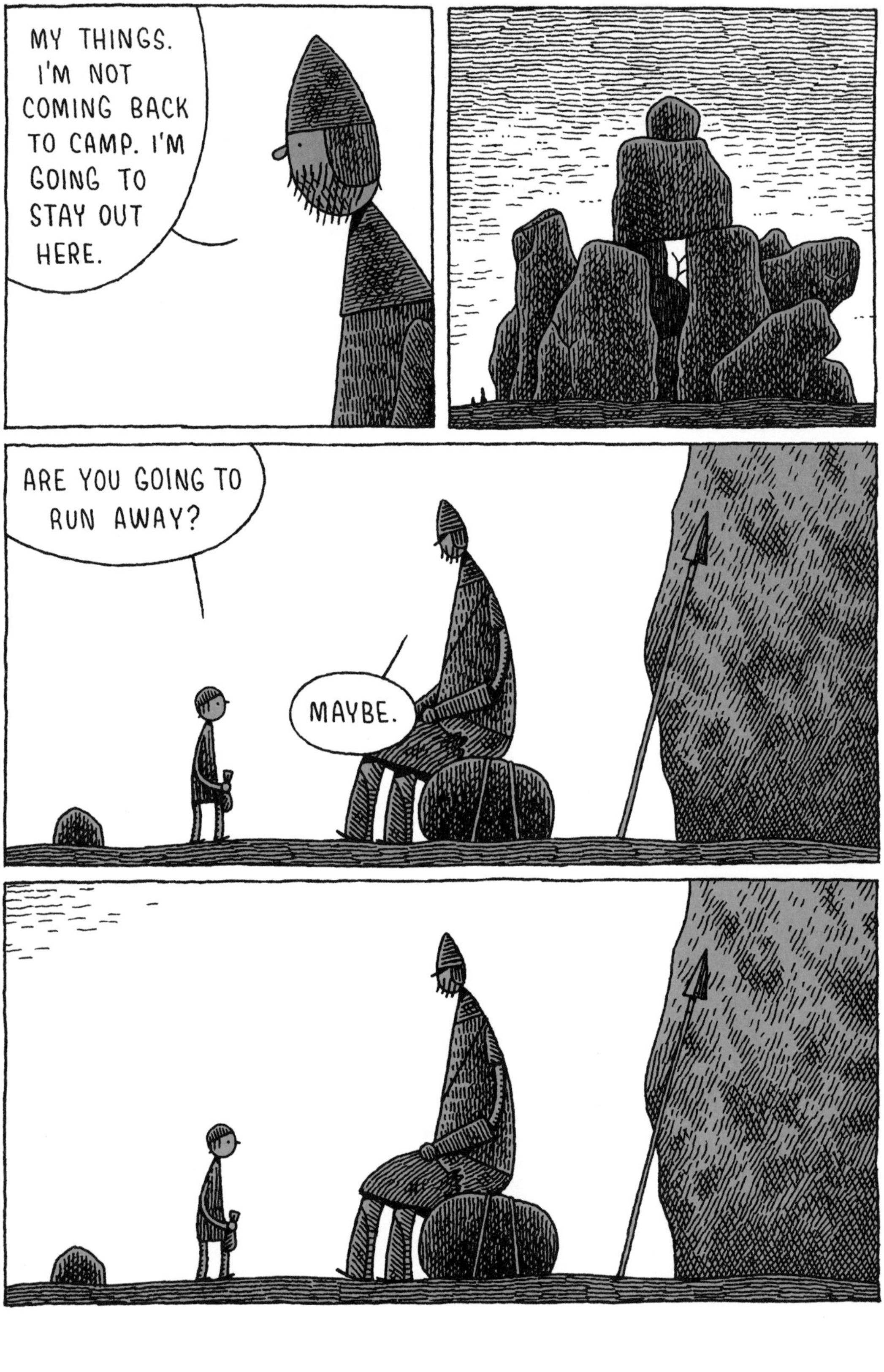
MY THINGS. I'M NOT COMING BACK TO CAMP. I'M GOING TO STAY OUT HERE.
ARE YOU GOING TO RUN AWAY?
MAYBE.

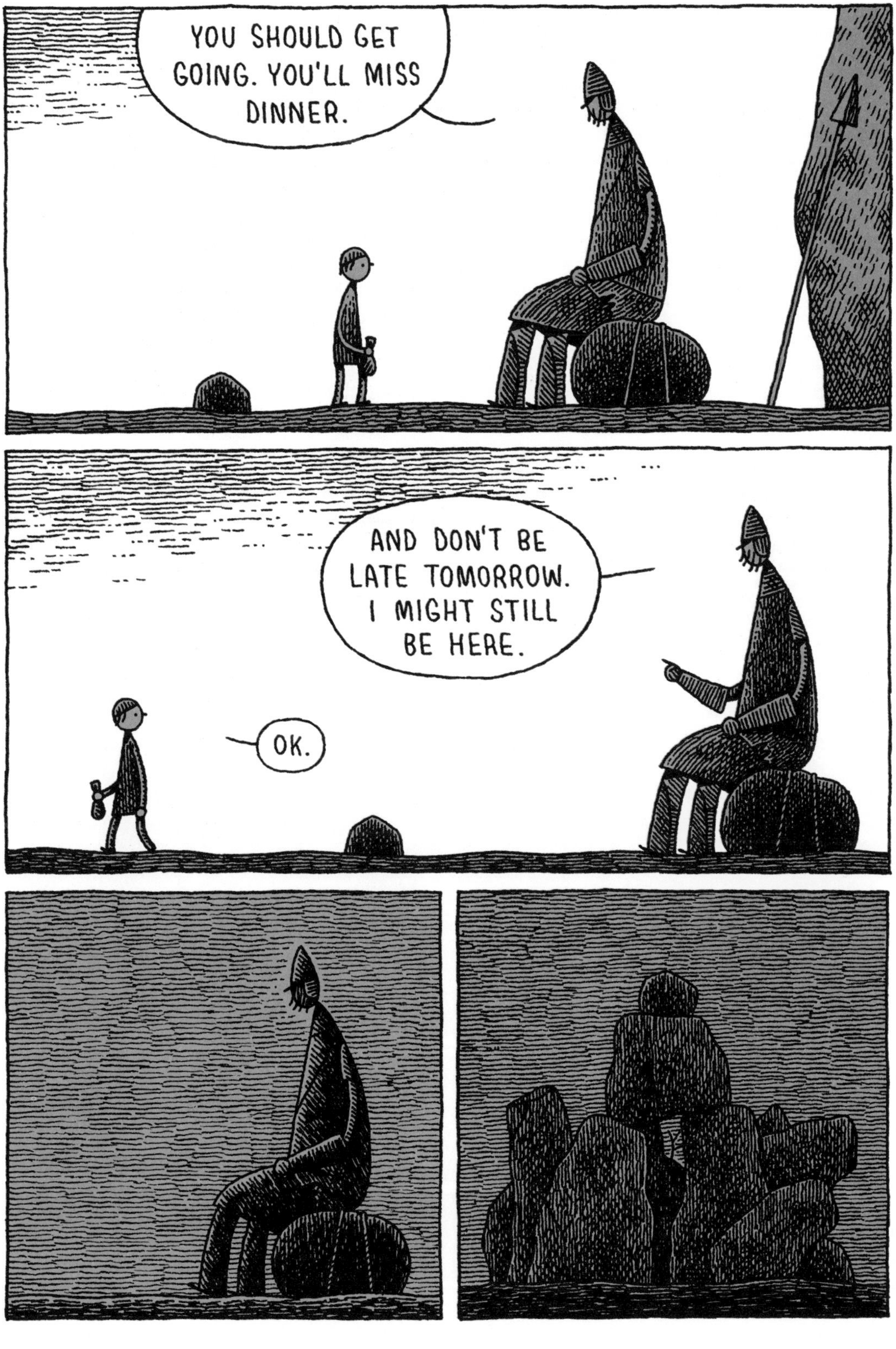
YOU SHOULD GET GOING. YOU'LL MISS DINNER.
AND DON'T BE LATE TOMORROW. I MIGHT STILL BE HERE.
OK.

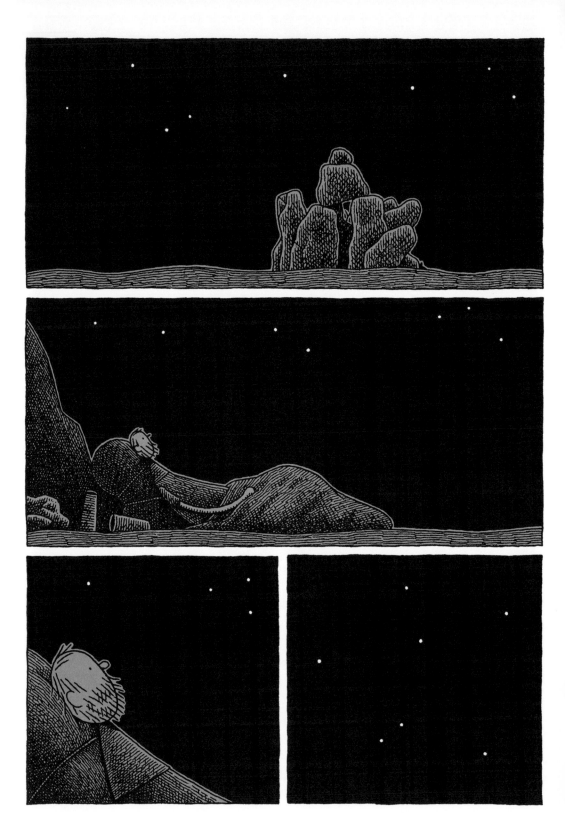

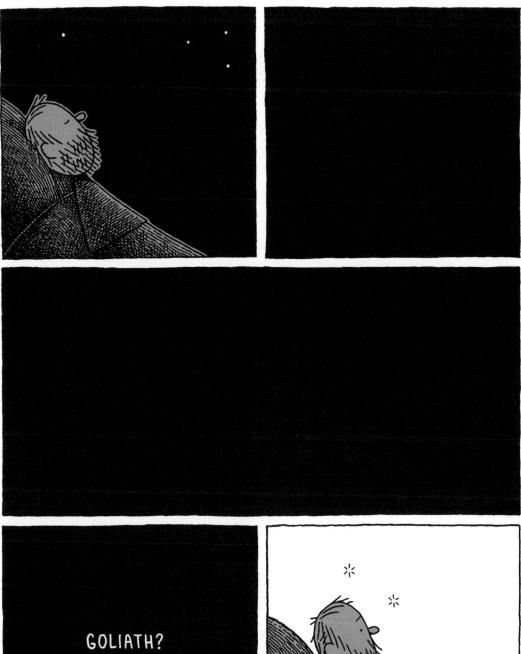

GOLIATH?

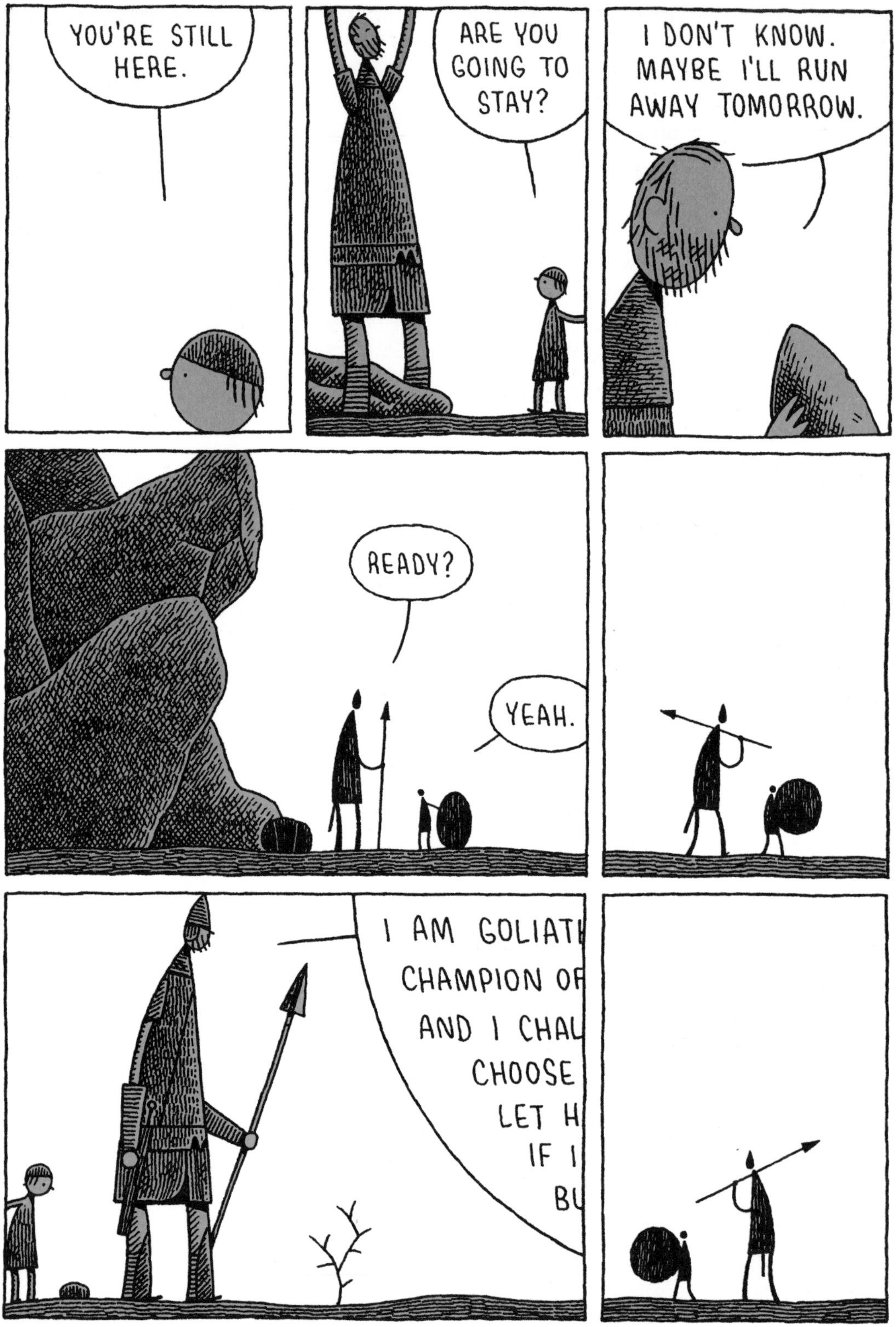
YOU'RE STILL HERE.
ARE YOU GOING TO STAY?
I DON'T KNOW. MAYBE I'LL RUN AWAY TOMORROW.
READY?
YEAH.
I AM GOLIAT
CHAMPION OF
AND I CHAL
CHOOSE
LET H
IF I
BU

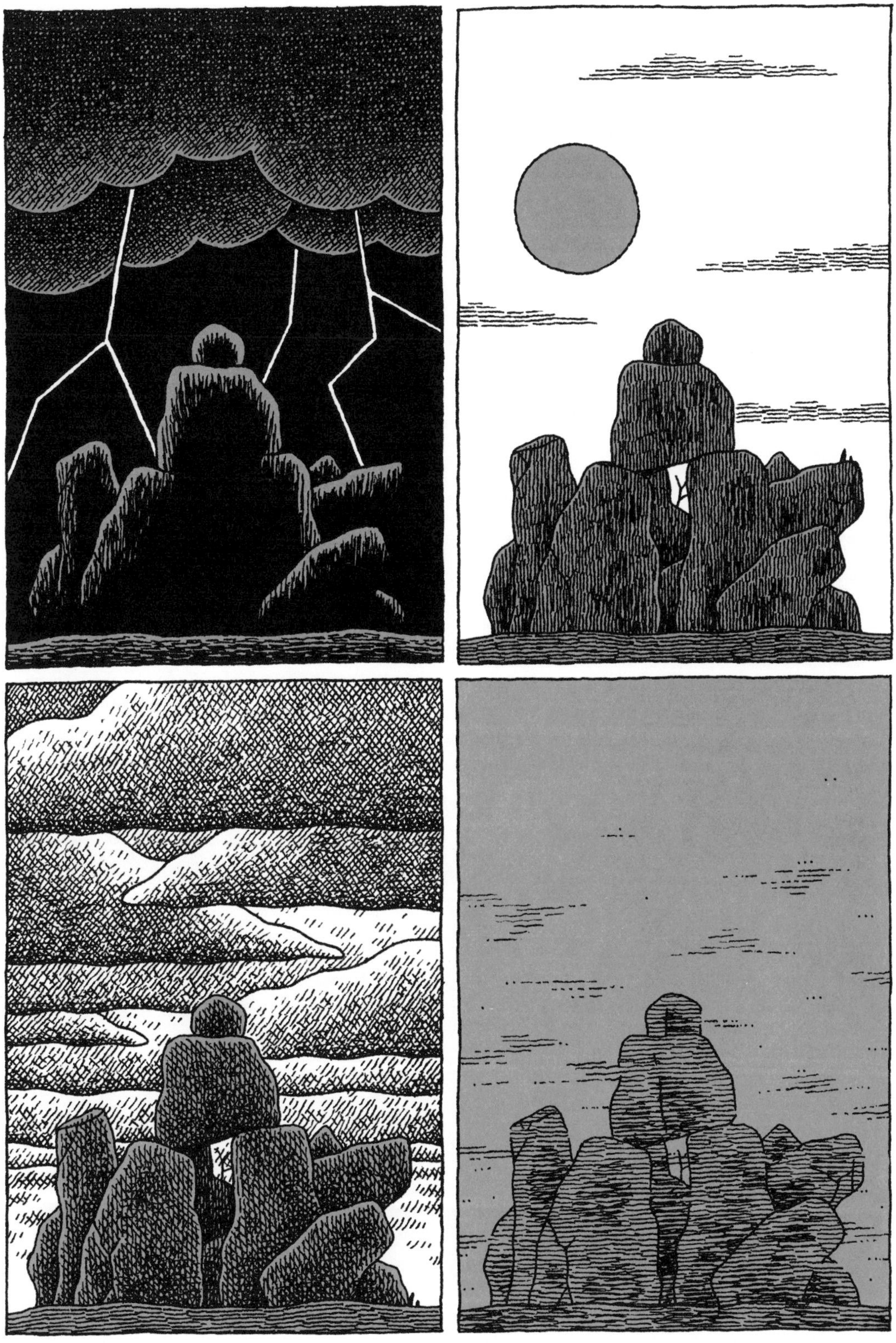

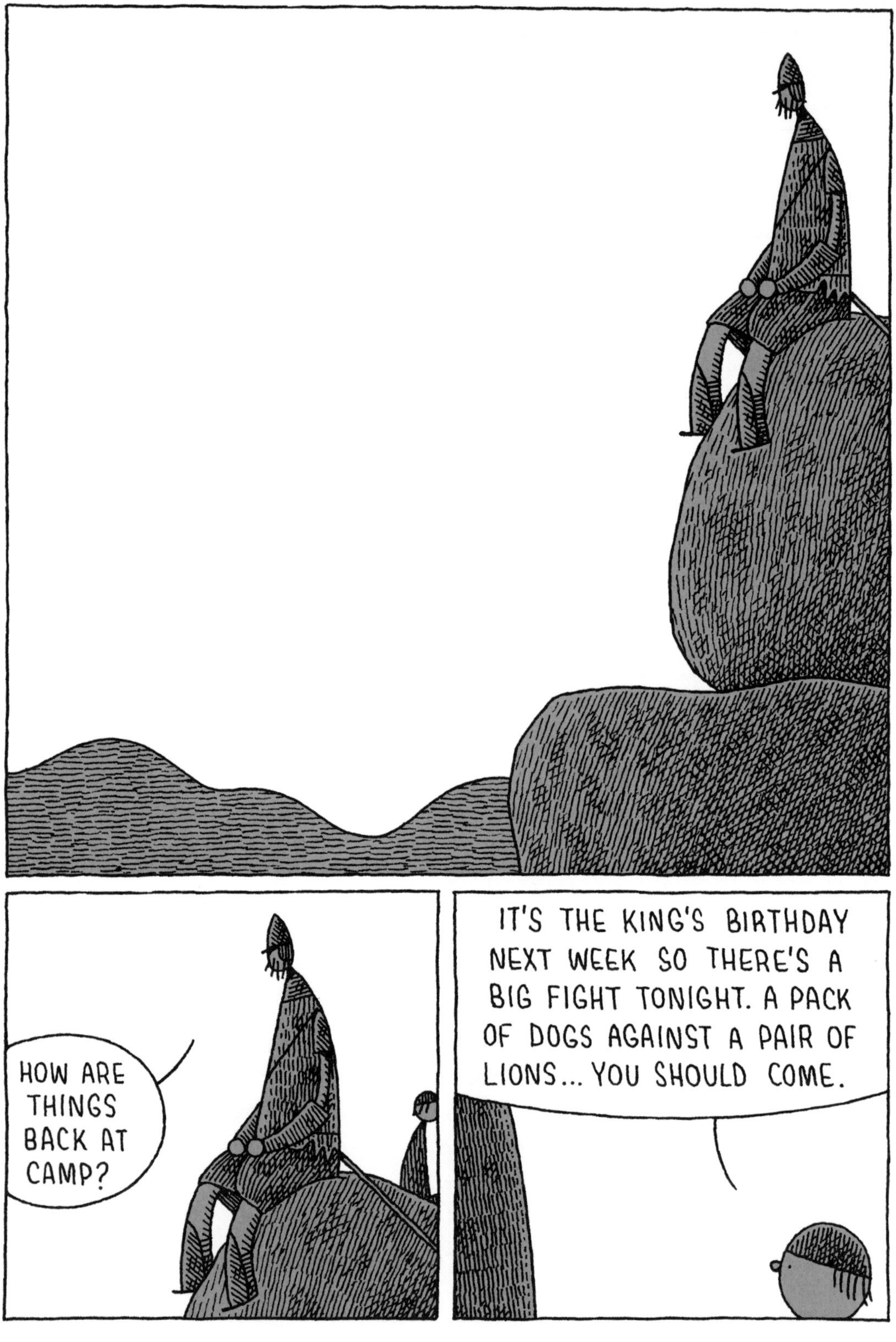
HOW ARE THINGS BACK AT CAMP?
IT'S THE KING'S BIRTHDAY NEXT WEEK SO THERE'S A BIG FIGHT TONIGHT. A PACK OF DOGS AGAINST A PAIR OF LIONS... YOU SHOULD COME.

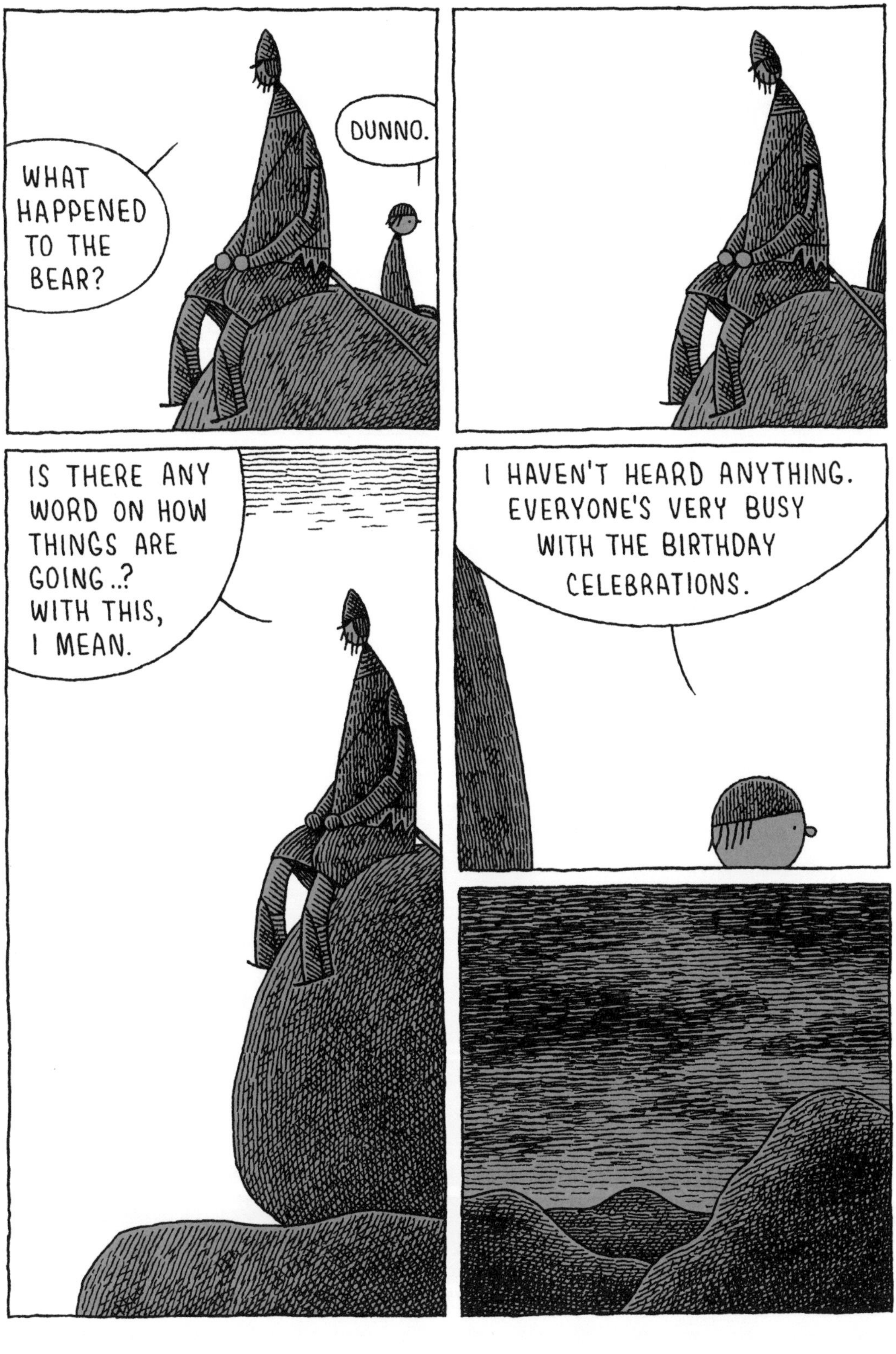
WHAT HAPPENED TO THE BEAR?
DUNNO.
IS THERE ANY WORD ON HOW THINGS ARE GOING..? WITH THIS, I MEAN.
I HAVEN'T HEARD ANYTHING. EVERYONE'S VERY BUSY WITH THE BIRTHDAY CELEBRATIONS.

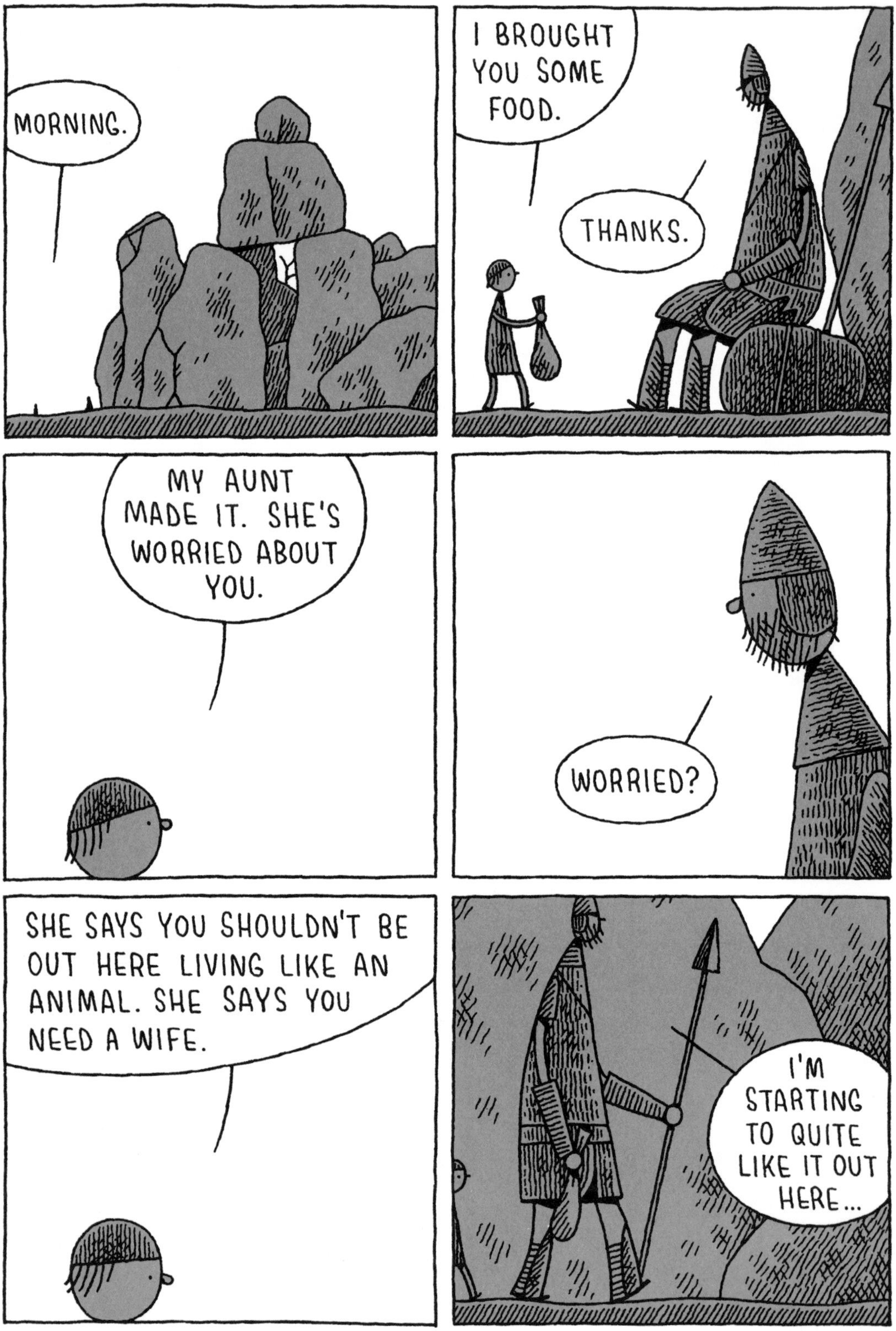
MORNING.
I BROUGHT YOU SOME FOOD.
THANKS.
MY AUNT MADE IT. SHE'S WORRIED ABOUT YOU.
WORRIED?
SHE SAYS YOU SHOULDN'T BE OUT HERE LIVING LIKE AN ANIMAL. SHE SAYS YOU NEED A WIFE.
I'M STARTING TO QUITE LIKE IT OUT HERE...

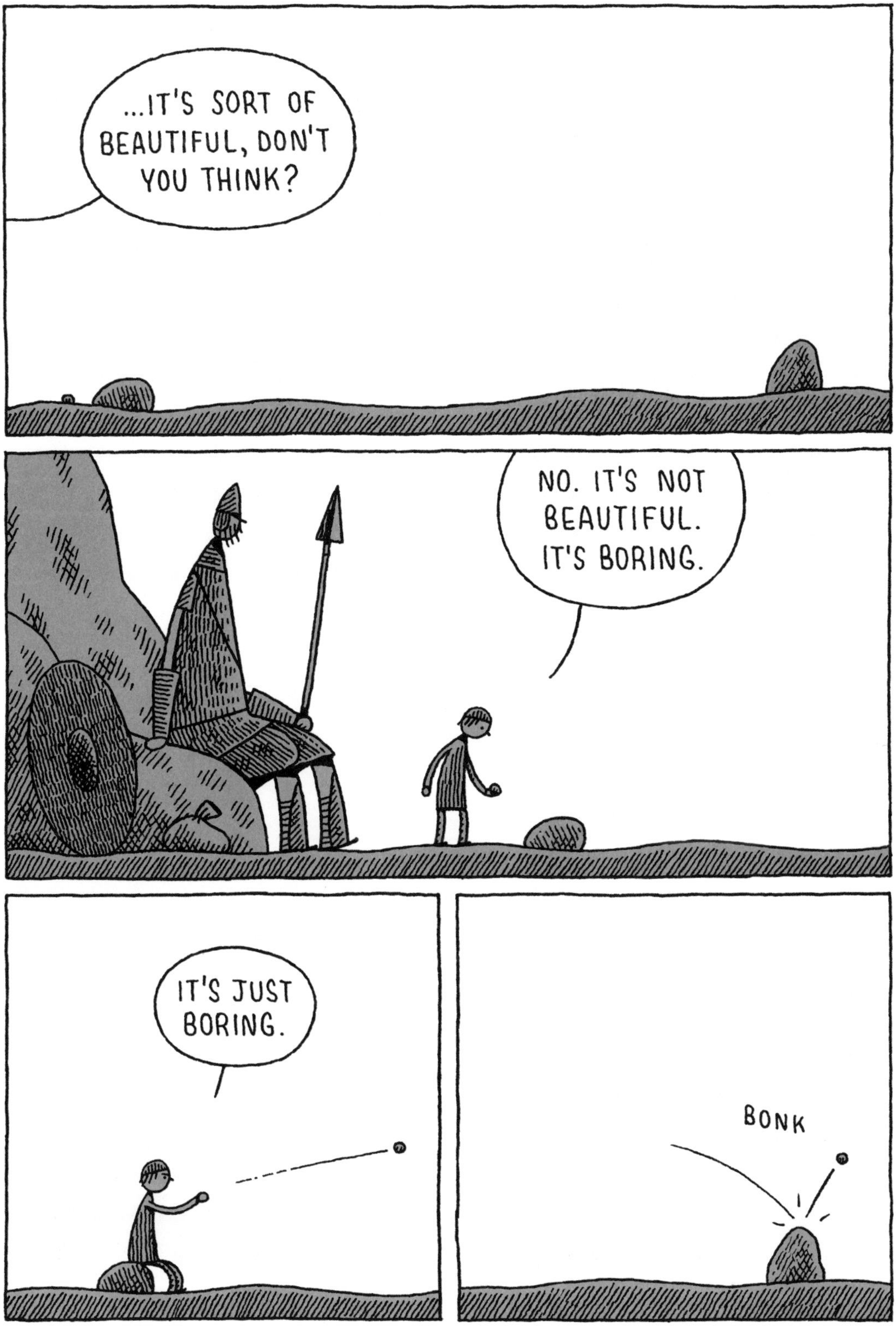
...IT'S SORT OF BEAUTIFUL, DON'T YOU THINK?
NO. IT'S NOT BEAUTIFUL. IT'S BORING.
IT'S JUST BORING.
BONK

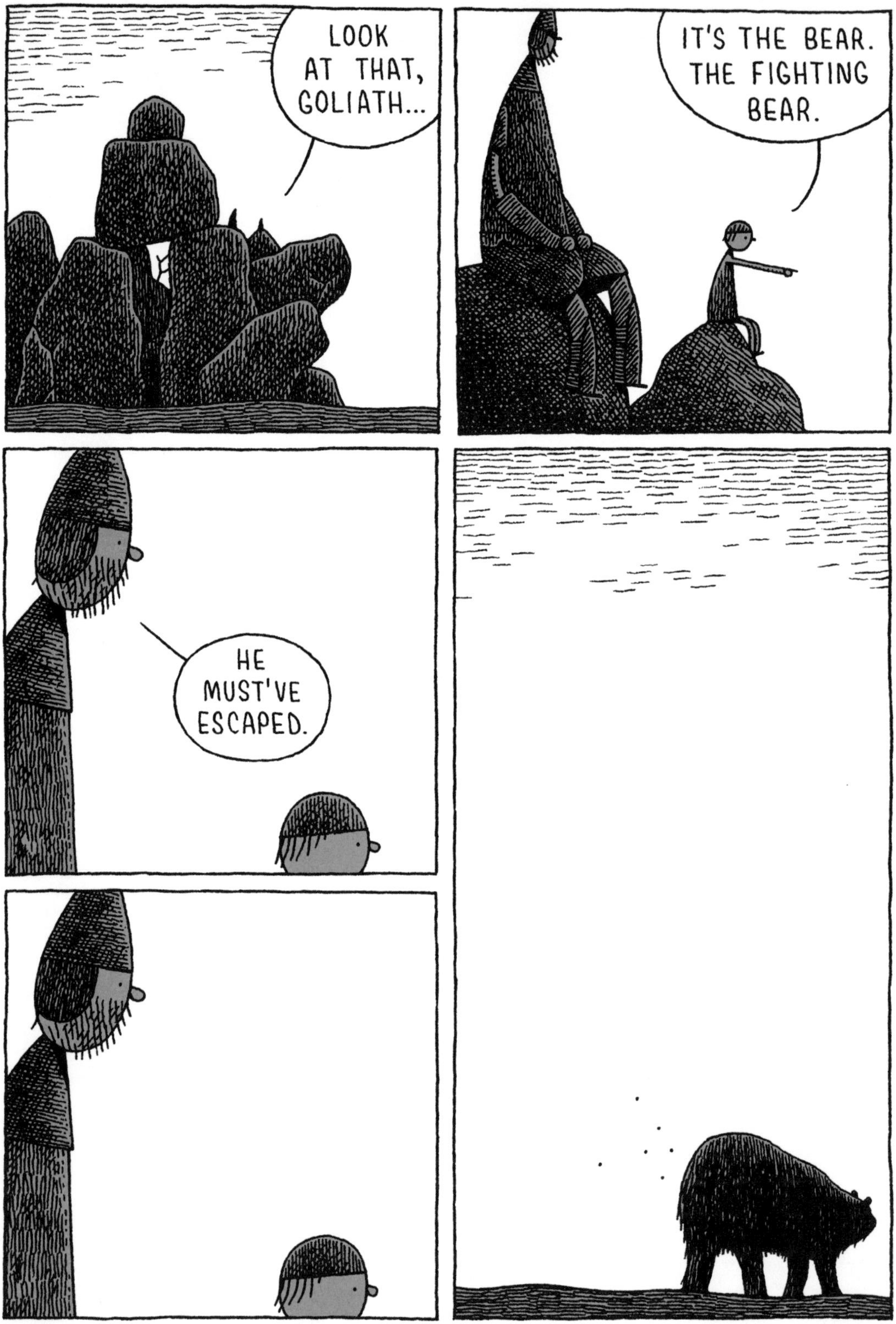
LOOK AT THAT, GOLIATH...
IT'S THE BEAR. THE FIGHTING BEAR.
HE MUST'VE ESCAPED.

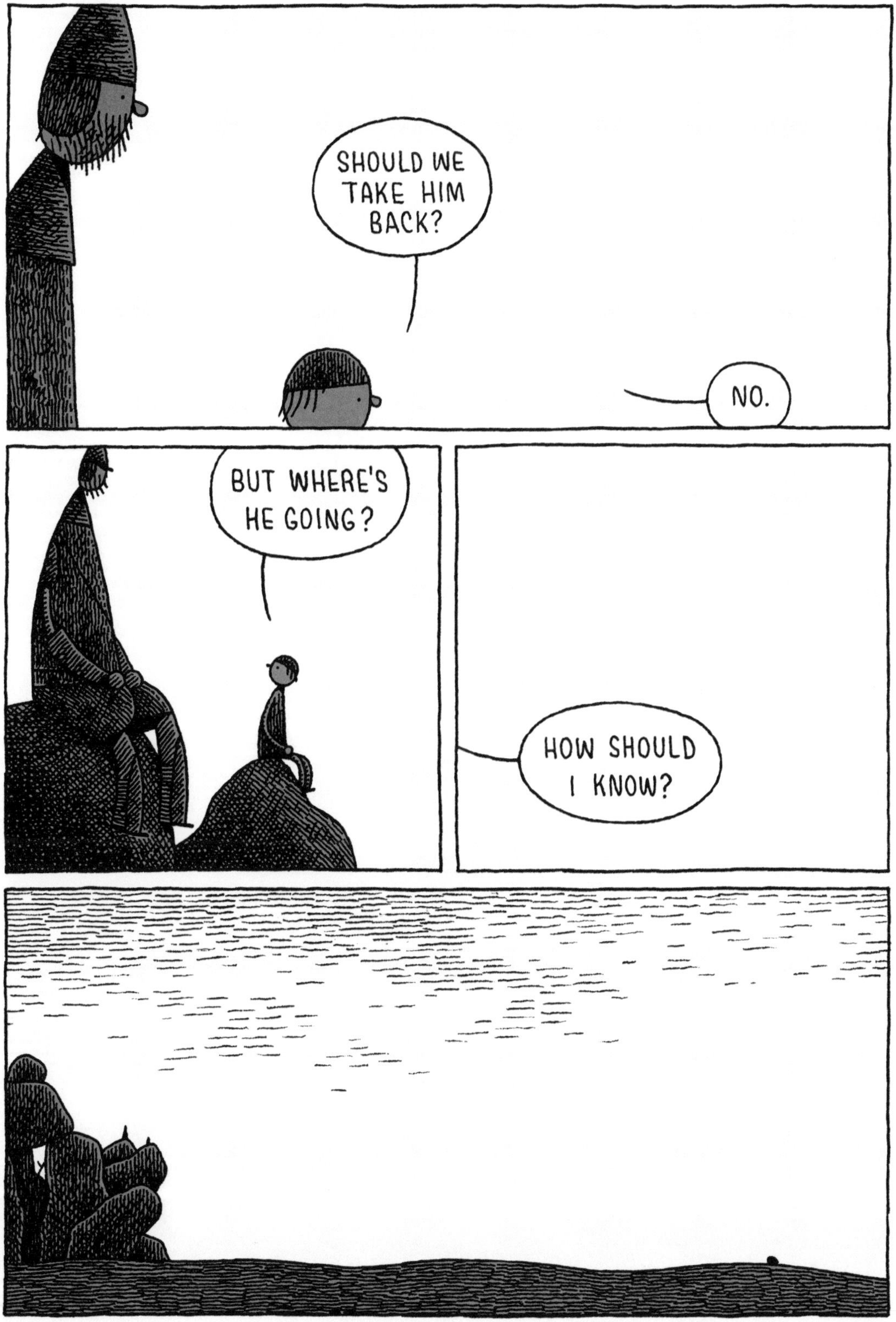
SHOULD WE TAKE HIM BACK?
NO.
BUT WHERE'S HE GOING?
HOW SHOULD I KNOW?

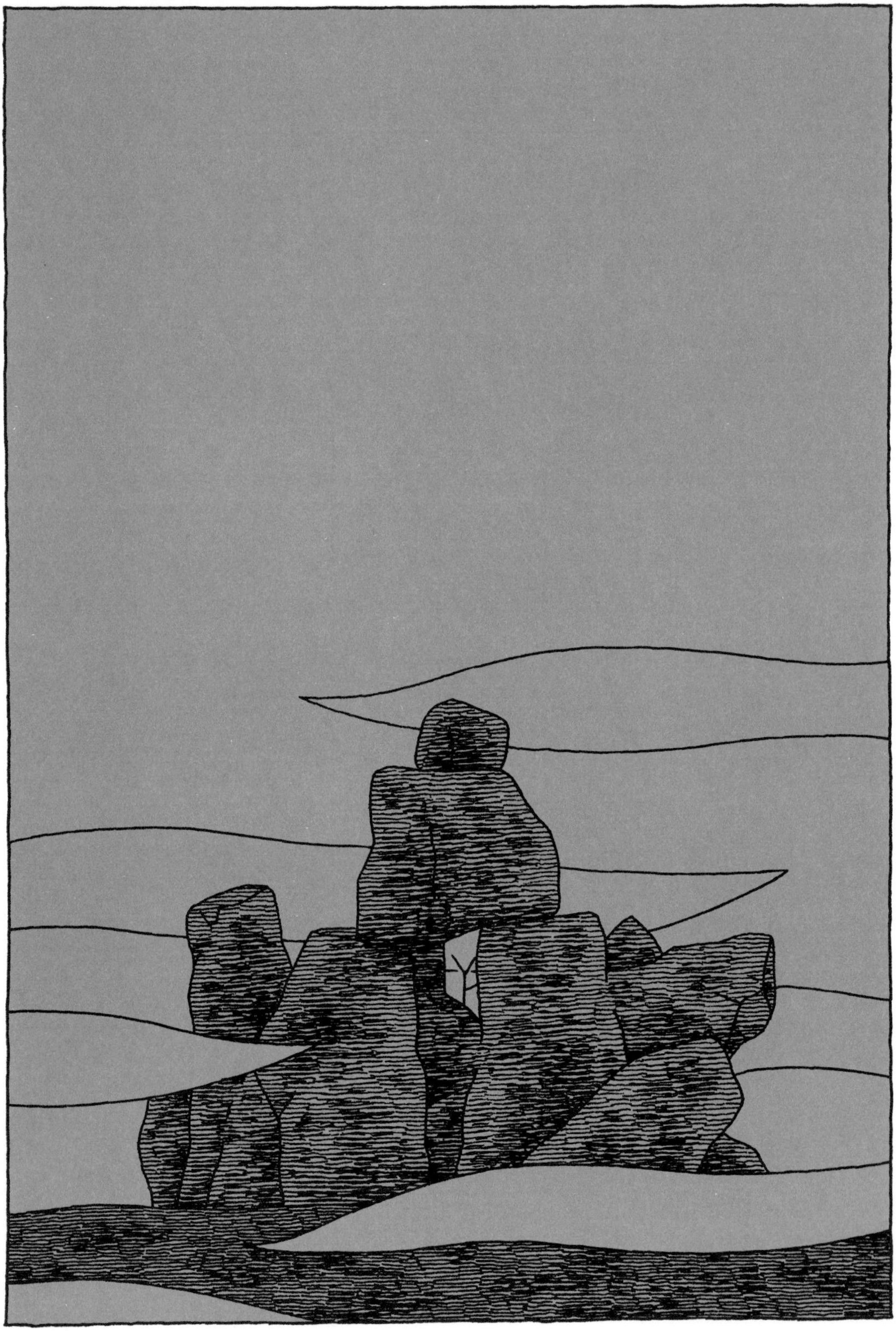

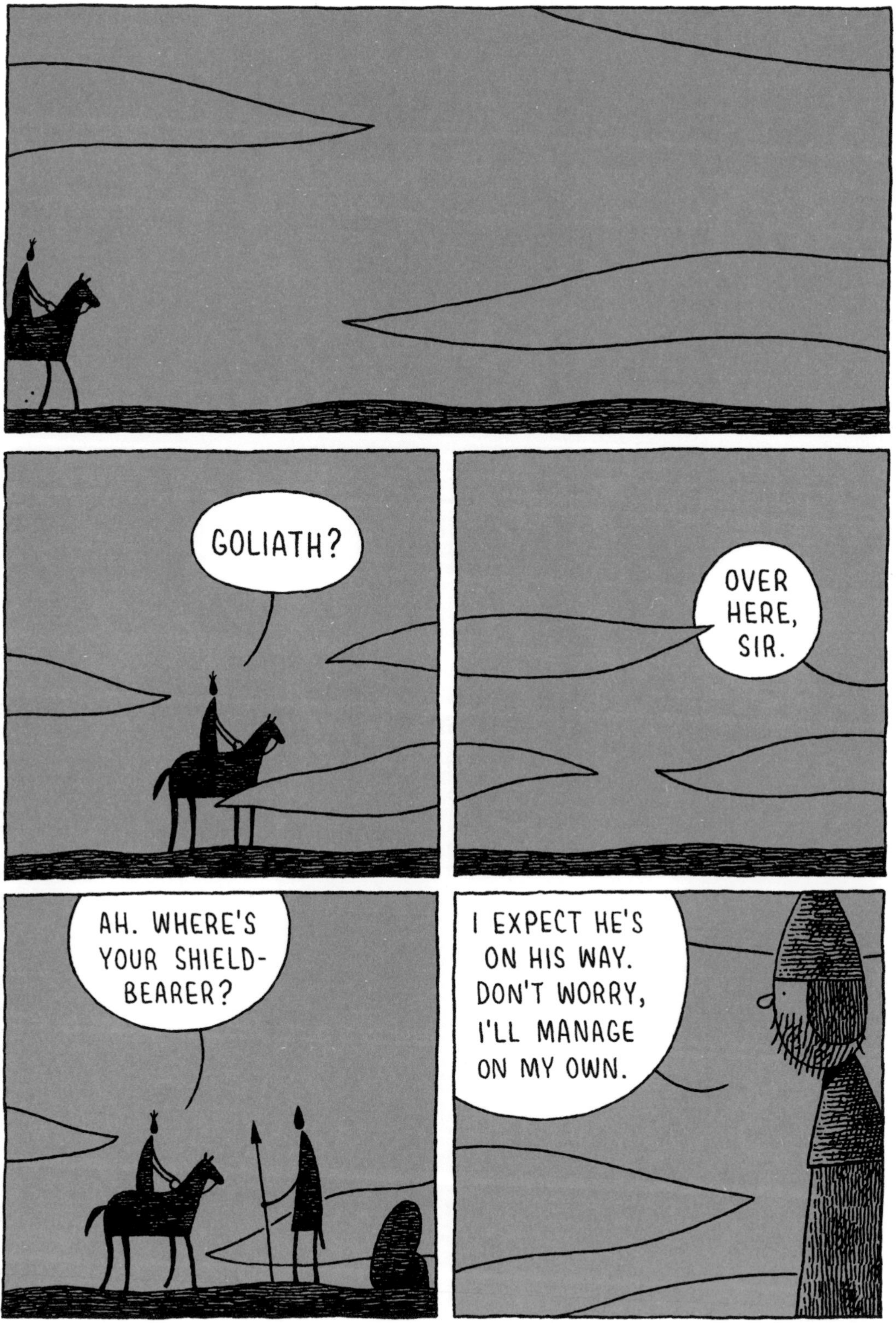
GOLIATH?
OVER HERE, SIR.
AH. WHERE'S YOUR SHIELD-BEARER?
I EXPECT HE'S ON HIS WAY. DON'T WORRY, I'LL MANAGE ON MY OWN.

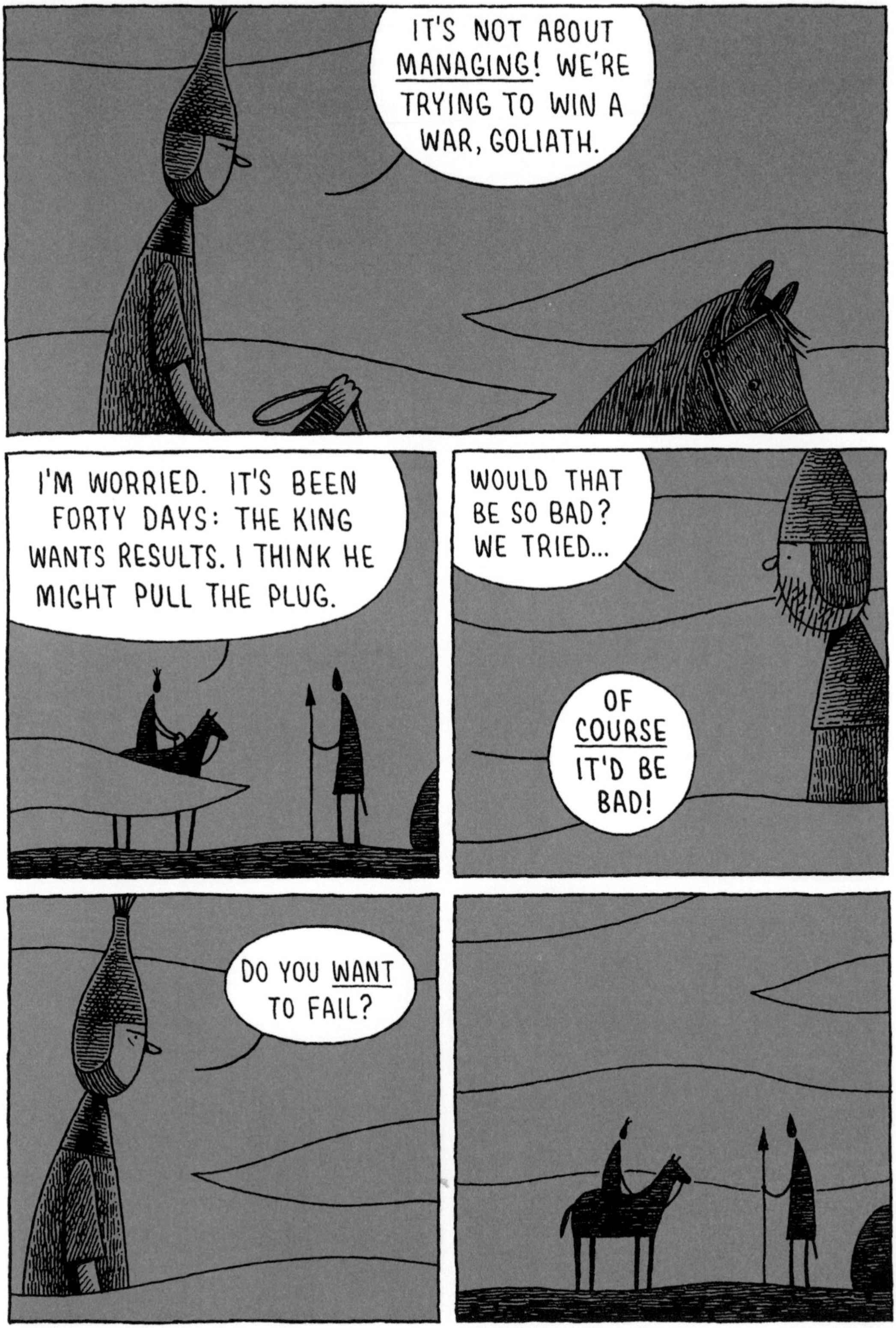
IT'S NOT ABOUT MANAGING! WE'RE TRYING TO WIN A WAR, GOLIATH.
I'M WORRIED. IT'S BEEN FORTY DAYS: THE KING WANTS RESULTS. I THINK HE MIGHT PULL THE PLUG.
WOULD THAT BE SO BAD? WE TRIED...
OF COURSE IT'D BE BAD!
DO YOU WANT TO FAIL?

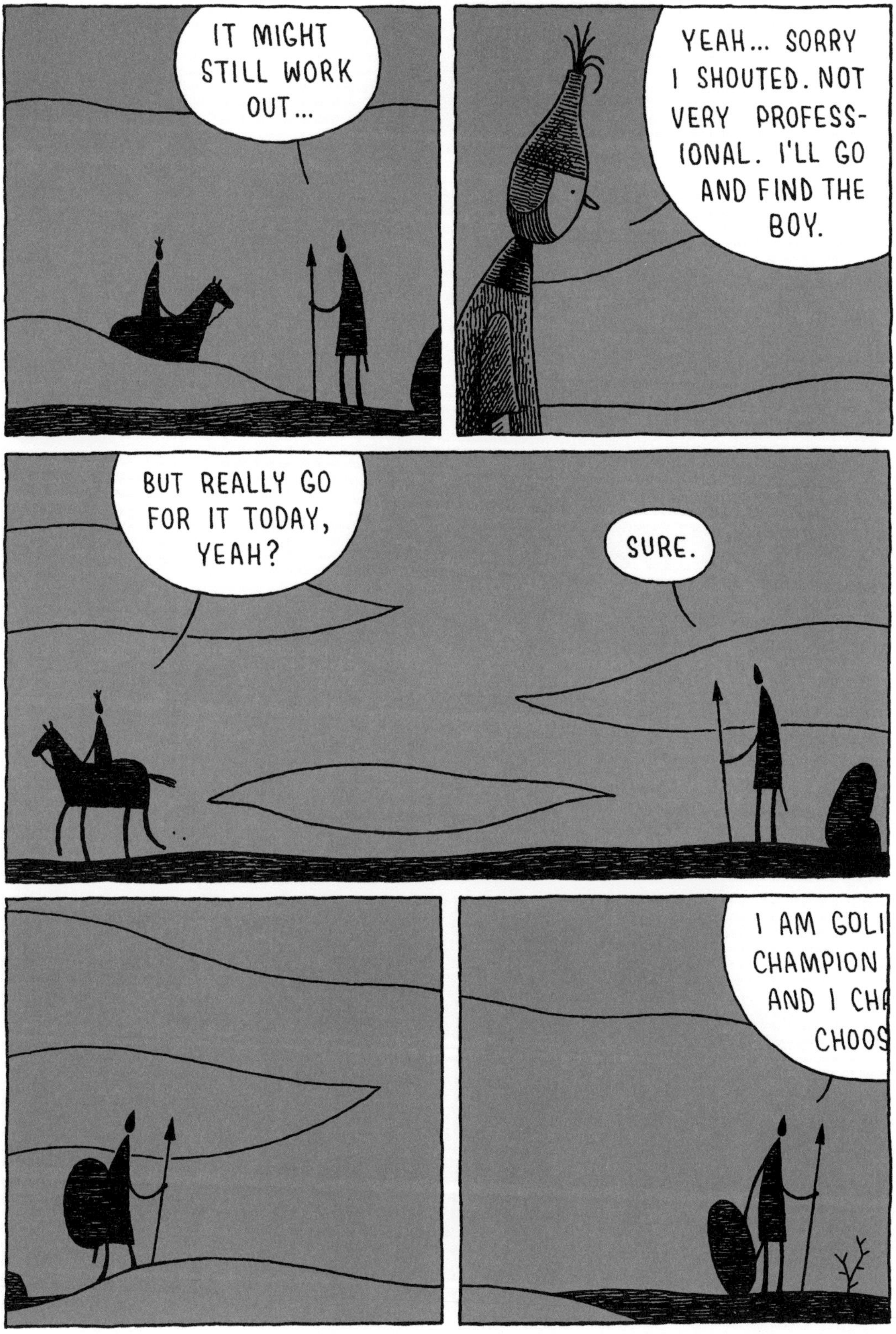
IT MIGHT STILL WORK OUT...
YEAH... SORRY I SHOUTED. NOT VERY PROFESS- IONAL. I'LL GO AND FIND THE BOY.
BUT REALLY GO FOR IT TODAY, YEAH?
SURE.
I AM GOLI
CHAMPION
AND I CH
CHOOS

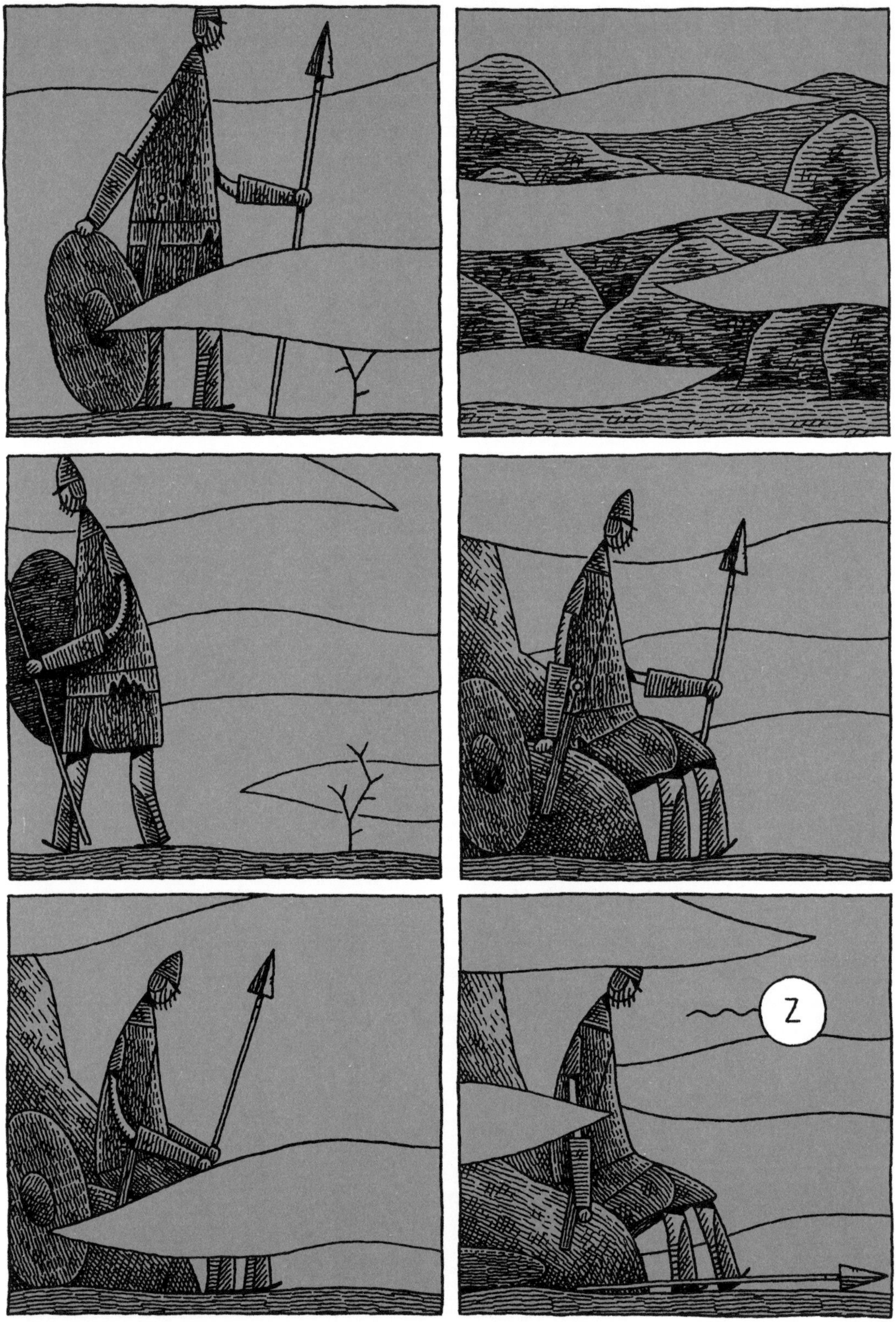
Z

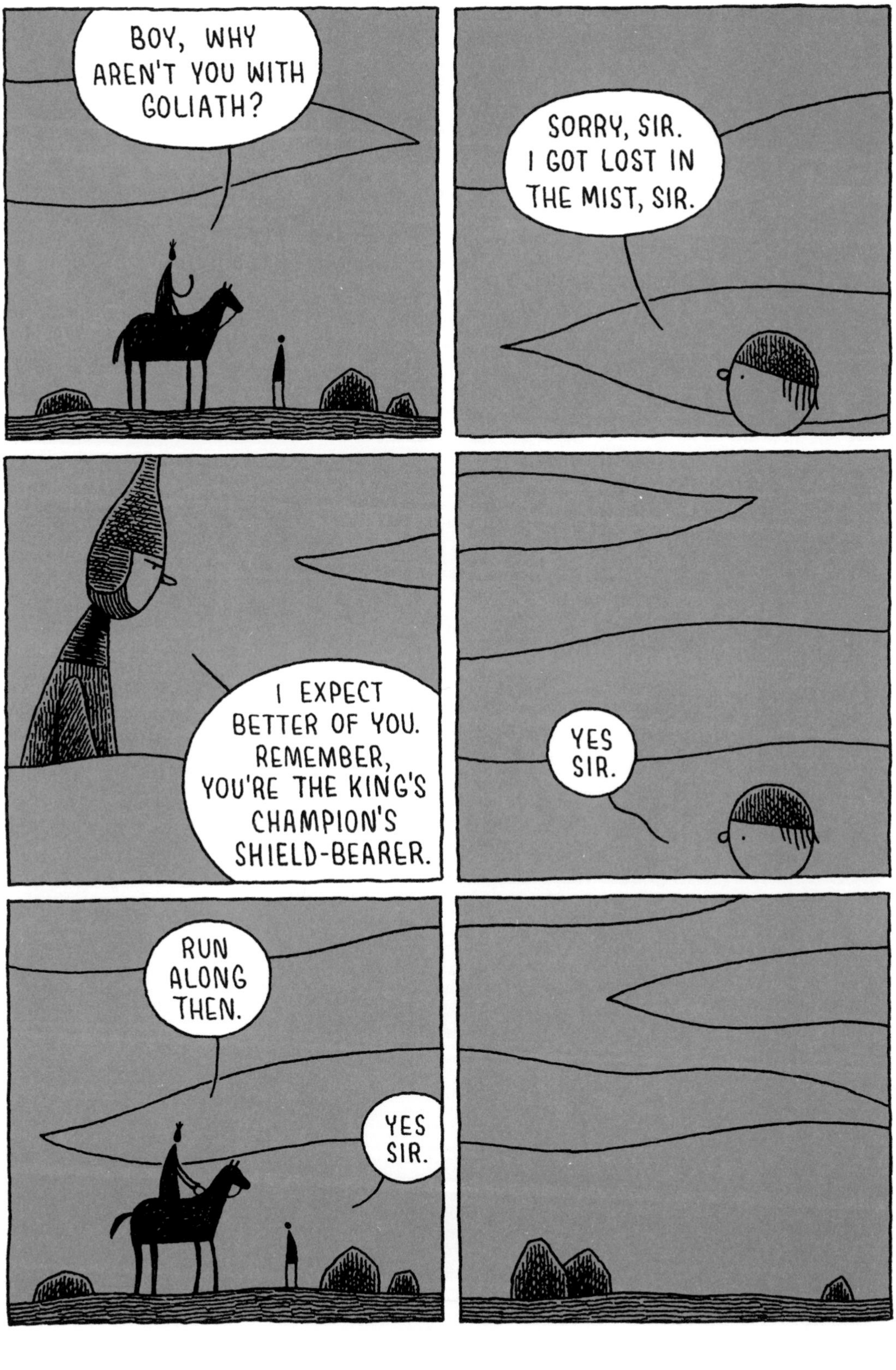
BOY, WHY AREN'T YOU WITH GOLIATH?
SORRY, SIR. I GOT LOST IN THE MIST, SIR.
I EXPECT BETTER OF YOU. REMEMBER, YOU'RE THE KING'S CHAMPION'S SHIELD-BEARER.
YES SIR.
RUN ALONG THEN.
YES SIR.

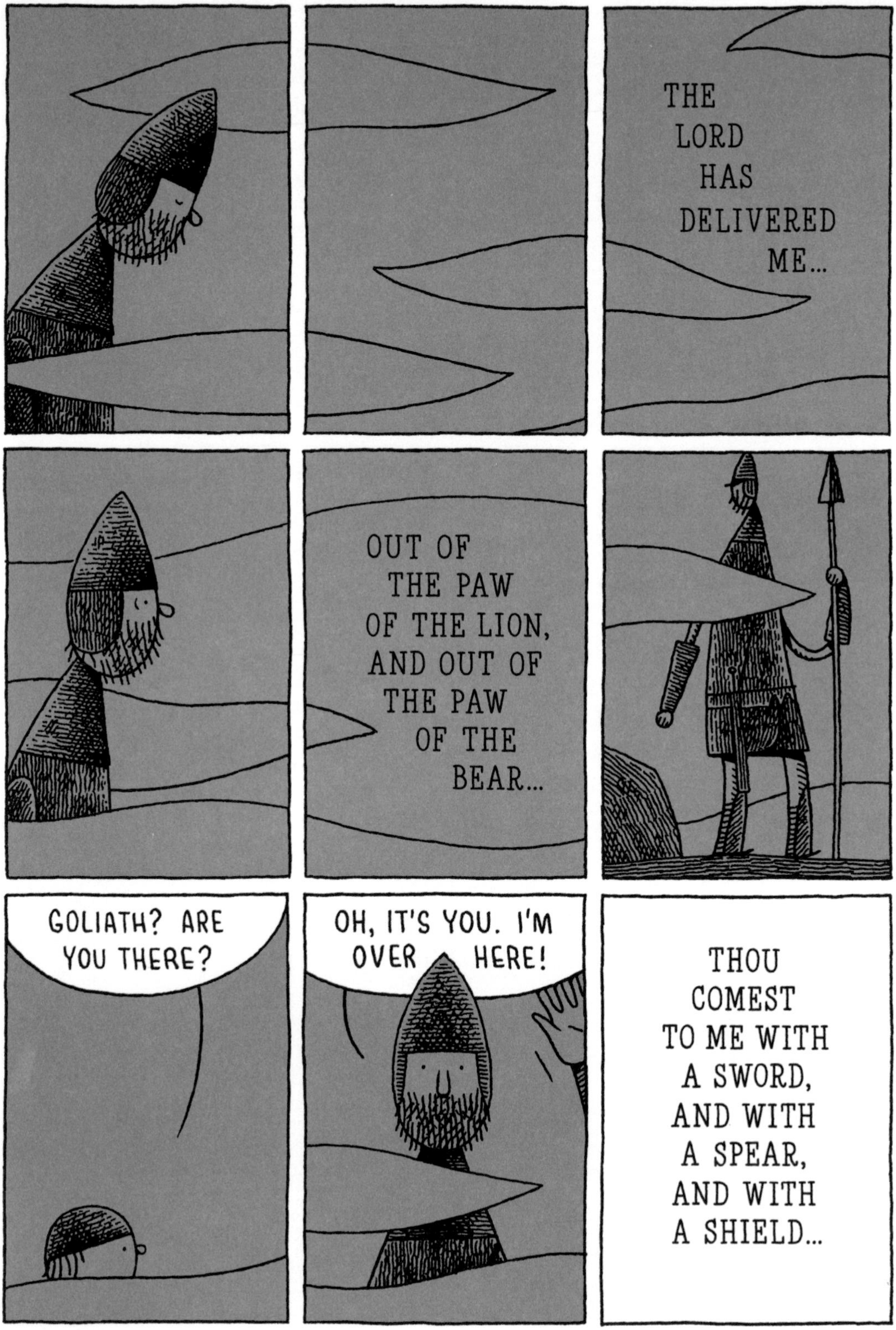
THE LORD HAS DELIVERED ME...
OUT OF THE PAW OF THE LION, AND OUT OF THE PAW OF THE BEAR...
GOLIATH? ARE YOU THERE?
OH, IT'S YOU. I'M OVER HERE!
THOU COMEST TO ME WITH A SWORD, AND WITH A SPEAR, AND WITH A SHIELD...

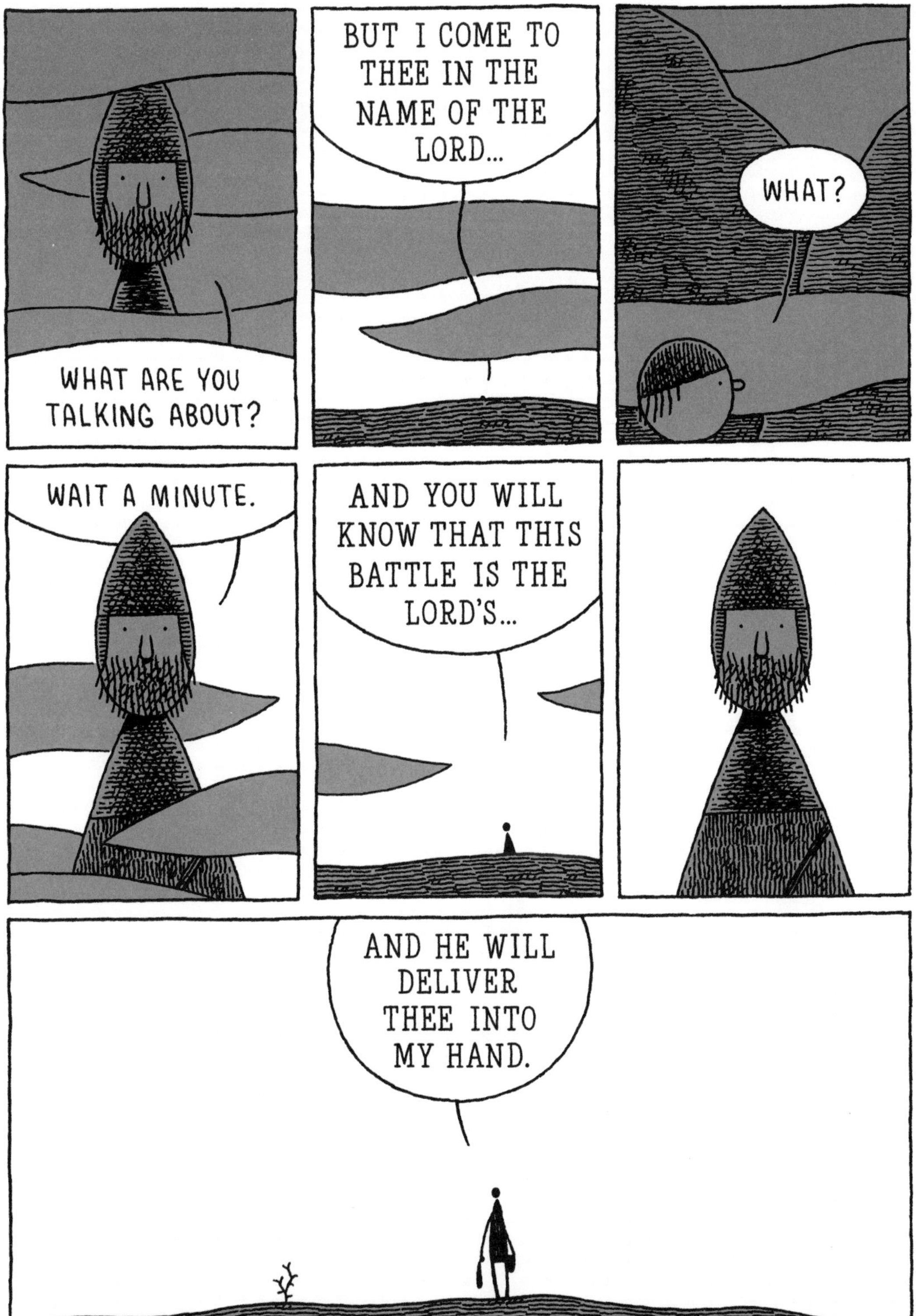
WHAT ARE YOU TALKING ABOUT?
BUT I COME TO THEE IN THE NAME OF THE LORD...
WHAT?
WAIT A MINUTE.
AND YOU WILL KNOW THAT THIS BATTLE IS THE LORD'S...
AND HE WILL DELIVER THEE INTO MY HAND.

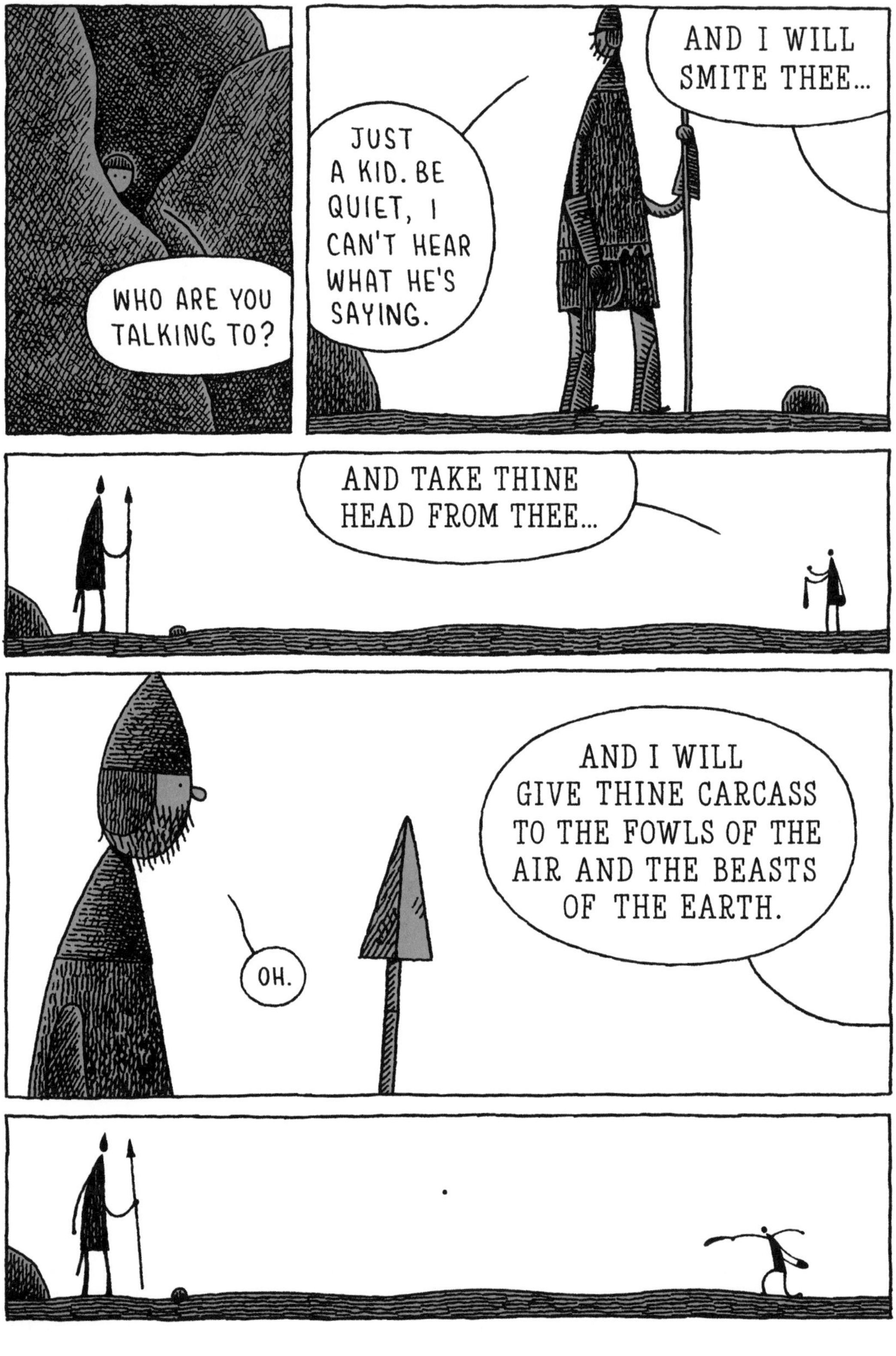
WHO ARE YOU TALKING TO?
JUST A KID. BE QUIET, I CAN'T HEAR WHAT HE'S SAYING.
AND I WILL SMITE THEE...
AND TAKE THINE HEAD FROM THEE...
AND I WILL GIVE THINE CARCASS TO THE FOWLS OF THE AIR AND THE BEASTS OF THE EARTH.
OH.

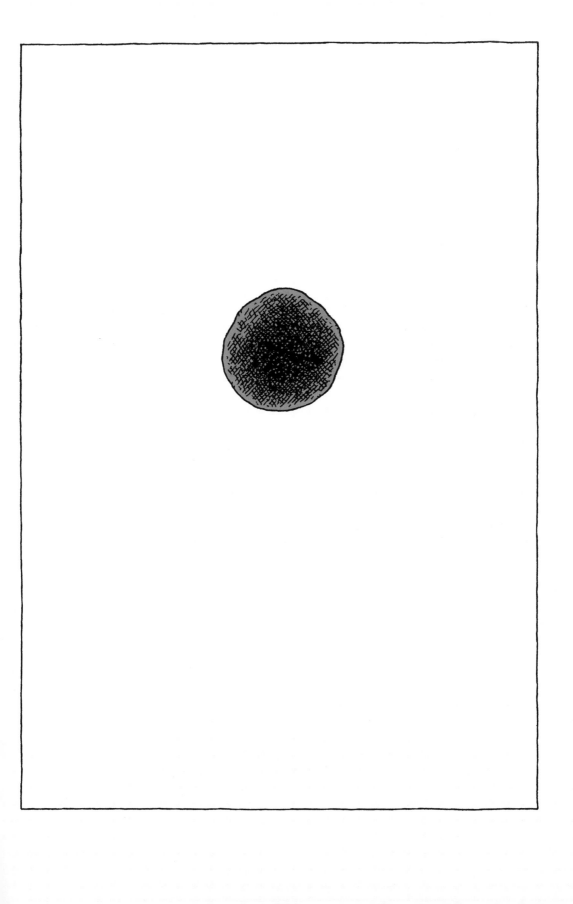

THUNK

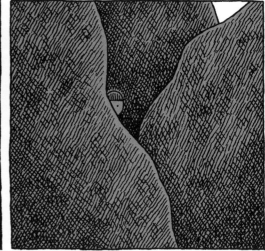

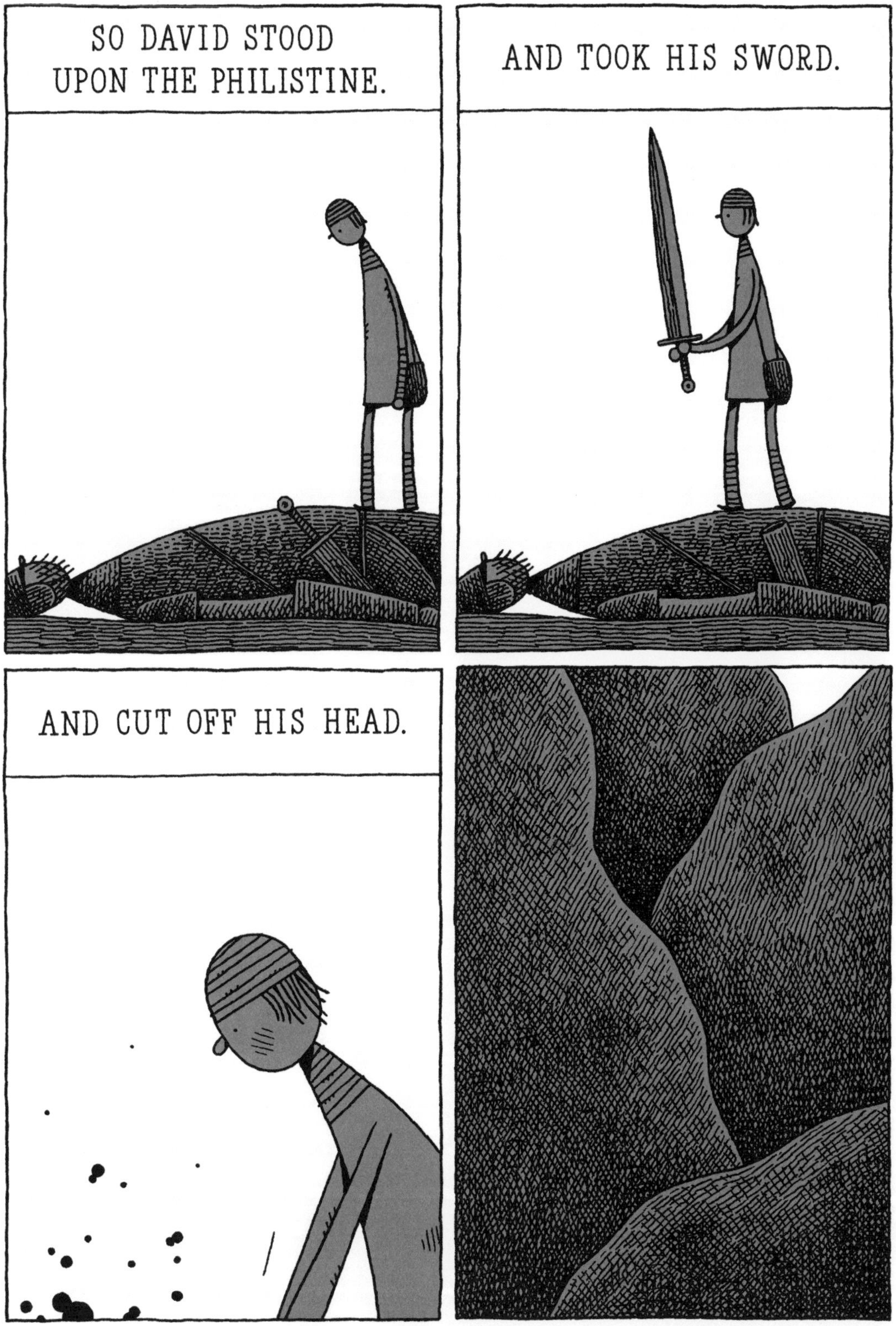
SO DAVID STOOD
UPON THE PHILISTINE.
AND TOOK HIS SWORD.
AND CUT OFF HIS HEAD.

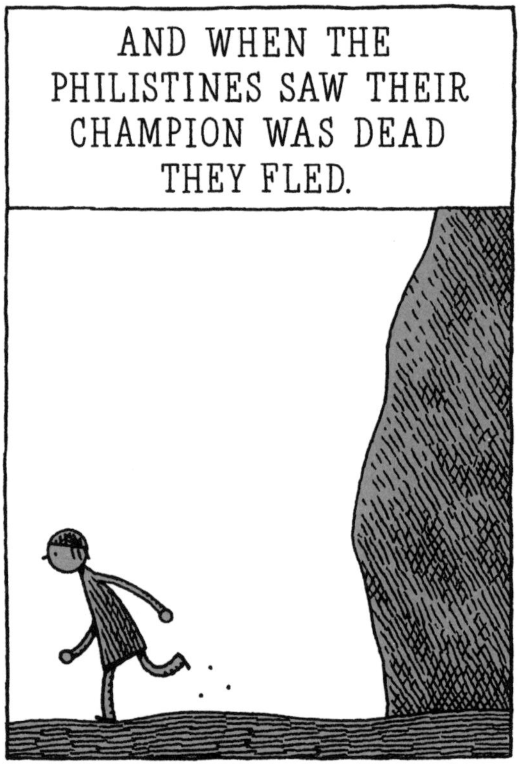
AND WHEN THE PHILISTINES SAW THEIR CHAMPION WAS DEAD THEY FLED.

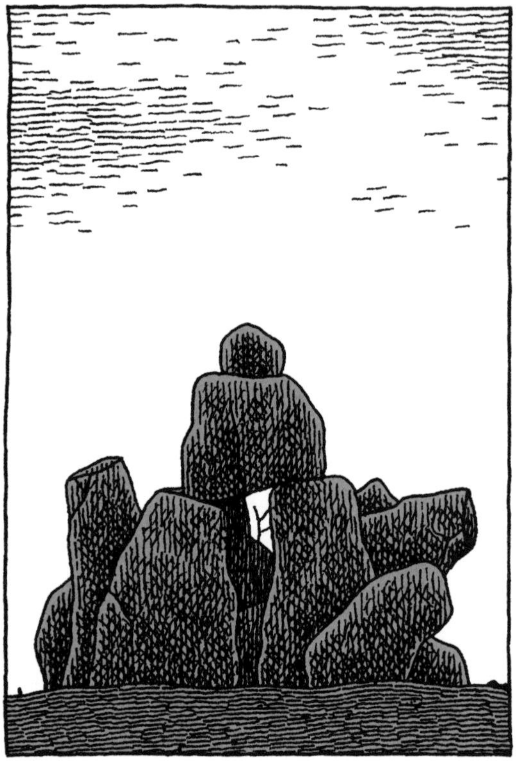

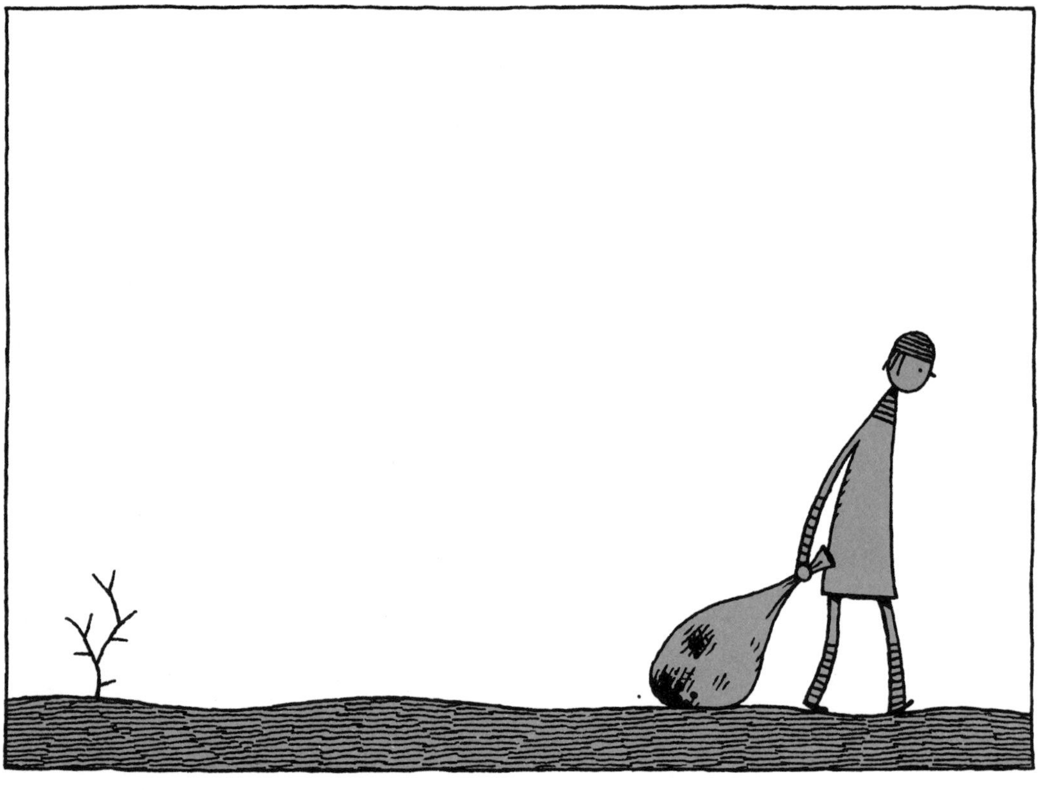

TOM GAULD WAS BORN IN 1976 AND
GREW UP IN ABERDEENSHIRE, SCOTLAND.
HE STUDIED ILLUSTRATION AT EDINBURGH
COLLEGE OF ART AND THE ROYAL COLLEGE
OF ART. HIS PREVIOUS COMICS INCLUDE
'GUARDIANS OF THE KINGDOM,' 'HUNTER
AND PAINTER' AND 'THE GIGANTIC ROBOT.'
SINCE 2005 HE HAS CREATED A WEEKLY
CARTOON FOR THE GUARDIAN NEWSPAPER.
HE LIVES IN LONDON WITH HIS FAMILY.

WWW.TOMGAULD.COM